the perfect peach

 Recipes and Stories from
the Masumoto Family Farm

the perfect peach

Marcy, Nikiko & David Mas Masumoto

photography by Staci Valentine

TEN SPEED PRESS
Berkeley

CONTENTS

FOREWORD

LIKE THE MASUMOTOS, all of us have our "peaches," don't we? At least those of us who have discovered a passion for something. We can point to the experience of that one special thing—that taste or trip, class or deal, project or play—after which life was different, *we* were different. A time when something was awakened within us that both fed us and challenged us, that so captivated us that we wanted to make it forever part of our lives and, feeding off our zeal, part of the lives of those around us.

I have no idea whether it's the nature of peaches themselves or mere coincidence, but my "peaches" moment came with peaches. Like most of us who came of age in the sixties, I was raised in a family whose grandparents still had tenacious, though eroding, roots in agricultural soil. Not farms for my Oklahoma City family, but big "victory" gardens of okra, tomatoes, and Kentucky Wonder green beans, foraging expeditions for sand plums, endless hours of cracking pecans from the tree at the back of the yard, dragging home can-able bounty from farm stands, and our yearly expedition to the Paul's Valley to pick peaches.

Peaches taught me some transformative lessons, certainly ones that are less complex than those they have taught to the Masumoto clan. They were an occasion for my sassy, red-headed, hourglass-figured Grandmother Potter to corral as many grandchildren as she could into her sleek-finned '62 Cadillac for the two-hour trip to the peach orchard. Oklahoma sun is blistering in July, much as it is in California's Central Valley, and the parched earth around the peach trees was always dry and cracked wide into deep fissures. Yet at eight or ten or fourteen years old, climbing like monkeys into the trees on rickety homemade ladders to collect enough of the aromatic fruit to fill seven or eight bushels was a thrilling adventure. Noisy adventure as we challenged each other to dangerous heights and unrealistic peach-picking speed. Torturous adventure by the end of several stiflingly hot hours wrestling with peach fuzz, mosquitoes, and pointy leaves.

Anyone who's bitten into a fully ripe, just-picked peach—hot from the summer's sun and ripe enough to be what the Masumotos call a "gusher"—knows that the feeling is completely, thoroughly arresting. Flavor that's exhilarating, even titillating; texture that's voluptuous and sloppy. At eight years old, eating peach after peach in the orchard was about nothing more than rampant consumption of forbidden sweets. At fourteen, for me, each peach stirred my newly awakening appreciation for the full range of sensual pleasures with which life abounds.

Sweaty and sticky and itchy from the fruit's fuzz, we grandchildren dragged the bushels to Grandma's car and fit them into her hot tub–size trunk, knowing full well that some would have to share the backseat with us. The ride back had each of us constantly jockeying to get close to the vents of the car's piddling air conditioner. The ride was worn-out quiet, but for me, every minute of it was pure pleasure. Two hours enveloped richly in the intoxicating aroma of ripe peaches. It was an aroma that would saturate every breath of the next several days. It was those sun-heated mouthfuls of peach that haunted my memories, that finally led me back to the kitchen as my life's work.

For days, we ate and breathed peaches. We peeled them to fit like jewels into jars, covered them with hot sugar syrup and slid them onto basement shelves to unearth for winter peach cobblers. We pickled and jarred them to serve with baked chicken. And we learned that nature's perfection embraces a wider swath than what they teach in most chefs' schools. Not every peach we brought into the kitchen was a stunner, right for cobbler or pickling. Blemished from hail or sunburn or our hard handling, these peaches were perfect for chunky jam or glowing-bright jam or velvety peach butter. All of which became my specialties.

I loved peeling peaches until the pads on my fingers puckered and shriveled from all the juiciness. I loved the feel of sweet perfumey steam puffing up from saucepans set on the electric coils of Grandma's modern new range. I loved taking complete charge of one taste our extended family would nourish itself with over the next year. At least at the beginning I did.

As the days wore on and my enthusiasm waned, I learned the lesson that accompanies practically anything having to do with food, from growing it to crafting it. It's wearying, back-breaking, feet-punishing work that requires digging to your very core for every bit of strength and spirit. "Quick and easy," the food preparation mantra of the last decade or so, seems all smoke and mirrors when you're facing honest-to-goodness food preservation or cooking for more than one or two. Yet the lessons of dedication, stamina, and steady eyes-on-the-prize are ones I summon daily. Peaches taught them to me.

And peaches taught me the virtue of an honest dedication to kitchen craft. As our family gathered around Sunday tables for months after summer's memory had faded, I knew the peaches we'd labored over had drawn them there, promising pleasure and that intangible experience of familial solidarity.

A peach—a juicy ripe one—can seduce anyone with its ethereal flavor and sensual texture. But that's just the beginning. That peach has so much more it wants to share, if we'll just listen.

—Rick Bayless

INTRODUCTION

Dating a Peach / BY MAS

THE ART OF EATING THE PERFECT PEACH: First raise to the mouth and the aroma enchants, anticipation is stirred. Insert in mouth and bite. Juices splash and squirt and you involuntarily lean over as the syrup drips down your cheeks and dangles on your chin. Flavors explode and the nectar dances across the taste buds. You slowly swallow and the aftertaste lingers and stays. Smack your lips and suck slightly on your tongue and a different wave of flavor delights. Memory is created. You lick your lips and pause before another bite, savoring the moment—slowly.

We are the Masumoto Family Farm, a fourth-generation family farm located twenty miles south of Fresno, in the heart of California. We live in the Central Valley, a fifty-mile-wide, four-hundred-mile-long flatland stretched between mountains. The Sierra Nevada tower to the east and provide us with snowmelt water, and the Central Coast Ranges lie to the west. We've been farming organically since the 1980s, part of the early wave of certified organic farms.

My grandparents emigrated from Japan as farmworkers and rented land in this valley. During World War II, the Masumoto family was relocated and imprisoned in a desolate internment camp because of their Japanese ancestry. My father bought the farm in 1948 and raised a family. Like many good farm kids, I ran off to college (University of California at Berkeley) but returned and started working alongside my father.

My wife, Marcy, comes from a family with German roots that settled in Wisconsin. Her folks came to California in the 1950s and operated a goat dairy where she was raised. She grew up milking the herd twice a day, every day. At least peaches take some of the winter off.

Our two children, Nikiko and Korio, grew up among the peach trees. College-educated Nikiko is taking over the family farm, part of a new generation on the land and a new role for women. Korio, still a college student, joins in and wisely claims, "I'll help my sister." They get along just fine.

The eighty-acre organic farm currently grows seven peach varieties and three nectarine varieties on twenty-five acres. Raisins are grown on thirty-five acres, and the remaining twenty acres are now part of a wild farm program, a nice way of saying "open" land. The critters love it; all farms should have something wild.

And we love peaches.

We're artisan farmers, working on a small scale, approaching work as craftspeople, engaging more as artists than as businesspeople. When we plow the earth, something is plowed into us. We live on our farm and draw no lines between our work life and family life. We farm stories.

We've spent a lifetime in search of the elusive perfect peach: touched by hands that are valued and grown in partnership with nature. What we've discovered is that great peaches crave attention. Each year we enter into a high-maintenance relationship that yields high rewards, some economic, others emotional.

It's like dating our farm's seven peach varieties (and three nectarine types) simultaneously. It's frequently exhausting, most of the time fulfilling, and occasionally confusing and humbling. But we don't have a choice: we are committed to a risky affair and take this calling seriously and responsibly.

The perfect peach from a farmer's point of view embodies the principles of organic and sustainable farming: socially just, environmentally responsible, and economically viable. The triple bottom line: people, planet, profits.

We strive to be responsive to our workers. Although we try to do most of the work ourselves, we do employ laborers. I can see my family in their faces; my grandparents and parents were also farmworkers. But today the language of our perfect peach necessarily includes Spanish, spoken when a small team of workers toils in our fields. This is the hidden backstory of produce and modern farming: farmers trying to balance the economic forces of costs and prices with the value of the hands that help grow and harvest their fruits.

On our farm, we employ organic farming methods, working with nature as much as we can. That means using no synthetic pesticides, developing a natural fertility program of compost and inputs, and a return to lots of hand labor by the family. We've made a million mistakes and lost crops: too naive to stop, too stubborn to quit, just dumb enough to believe we can make this natural approach to modern farming somehow work, always believing the future will be better. A neighbor once joked with me that following the death of an old farmer, they did an autopsy and found he was full of "next years."

Our method of farming requires lots of hours walking our fields. We began by building the soil, increasing organic matter, and wanting grasses (and weeds) to populate the landscape. We hope to grow life on the farm.

Yet we can't continue to farm without gain—without enough profits to keep us in business, enough rewards to sustain us into the future. It wasn't the plan, but the farm began as a nonprofit operation. We then quickly learned a real farm has real expenses, that good intentions do not pay bills. If we could not sustain our work and vision, real change could not occur.

Farming timelines have to be measured in decades, if not generations. We have had some success, found good homes for our peaches and ideas, at times discovered off-farm income adds needed stability. And we've gotten a little smarter, too. We hoped to move forward with social, cultural, and political transformations in agriculture and learned that it can't happen in a single year.

On our family farm, the perfect peach has evolved into something more. We believe farming must also have a public face: we want to tell the story of who grows produce, how it's grown, and why it should be part of the flavor spectrum. Food and farming belong in the public arena. Our farm is not an anonymous factory in the fields. Peaches should not become a commodity that you cook with or eat out of hand without knowing the story behind them. All of our peaches are for public consumption. We strive to be transparent about how we work, how we live, and how we cook, including the shortcomings and mistakes.

Finally, we insist that passion becomes part of the essence of our fruits. We take this all personally, perhaps too personally. But it's the nature of caring and engaging that has become the mantra of our farm. This is all about peaches from a farmer's point of view, a perspective that necessarily includes the farm family and its intimate relationship with the land. People. Planet. Profits. Public. Passion. And in the end, we hope that the perfect peach is one that is shared.

Our cookbook explores these ideas and inspires cooking and sharing peaches. We are passionate about our peaches but also realistic: farming is both romantic and real, and you must have both to survive and sustain yourself. On the farm, as we work, we often talk about authenticity, and we strive for that sensibility to be conveyed in these pages.

We've divided this book into sections, with both tension and pleasure as part of an unfolding story of a real family farm. After our introduction and a peach primer, we begin with sweat and thirst, welcoming you to our working family farm. We really do sweat on the farm, refreshed by quenching beverages.

Next, we gather at the family table, a table filled with stories of working the land as a family, along with the food that brings company together, and share savory recipes. We enjoy long meals at the farm, the perfect pairing of great food with great conversation.

Of course, our farm is not only about work. We also dream and we pause to enjoy the pleasures of life with luscious peaches. The sweetness of desserts blended with the fantasy of owning a working family farm—it doesn't get much better than these moments.

Finally, we end with memories and the art of preserving both peaches and the legacy of the family farm. Through preserves, like freezing, drying, and canning, we can taste a great peach in another season. We want to rekindle fond memories of harvests past and renew the spirit of tastes to come.

We hope that you enjoy this tour of our farm through recipes and stories and this journey into the taste that springs from our small piece of land. Welcome to the Masumoto Family Farm and our peaches.

Learn to Love a Peach / BY NIKIKO

We are in love with peaches. But we are not the first people to see a connection between peaches and matters of the heart. The metaphoric linkages have been made in popular culture (my generation might think of "Peaches & Cream" by 112, and baby boomers like my parents remember Peaches & Herb singing "Reunited and it feels so good"). Many of these references are amusing, but when it comes to living, working, and cooking on our farm, we actually try to live an earnest version of peach love.

This peach love, and consequently this book, is not really about perfection—or rather it is, but it's a different kind of perfect: a perfect dressed in hand-me-down clothes that pass from generation to generation. Maybe there is no preexisting perfect peach. Instead, maybe a peach becomes perfect when it reminds us of the deep connections that are already present when we eat one. Maybe a perfect peach wakes us up through our senses to listen, appreciate, and champion the ways in which we are interdependent as farmers, workers, cooks, and eaters. It's this perfection-in-process that I seek.

Every harvest, I envision the path of each peach as it leaves the farm, travels, and eventually goes home in someone's grocery bag or rests on a plate at a restaurant. Maybe it's yours? When that peach touches your lips and nourishes your body, I hope you feel love. Not a plastic-perfect or one-night-stand love. I want you to feel a deep reverence for the food that binds us with one another and the earth. I want you to hunger for our stories. I want you to help make all people in our food system equal partners. I want you to love us, too.

On our farm, we Masumotos do not love lightly, and it's not always pretty. We experience heartbreak, anger, infatuation, frustration, stillness, loss, and euphoria with our peaches, recipes, and orchard work. Farming is a struggle just as much as it is fulfilling (there is no beginning and no end), and our story is only part of the interdependent world of how we feed ourselves. We hope you can taste all of that in every bite.

A strong sense of place anchors this book. We grow peaches in the Central Valley of California. The geography of this place frames who we are, how we farm, and what we eat. Social histories of immigrants, resilience, neighbors, and hard work make up the soil of our farm and stories. We have worked to make these dynamics visible in the flavors and breadth of the recipes we've included. Just as the lives of farmers and farmworkers must be embraced in our dream of a sustainable food system, so too must the culture of the people in our valley be part of our concept of *terroir*. This is by no means a comprehensive peach book. We offer what we know now, from our lives in Del Rey, California, and hope that the journey of growth continues as we meet on the page, in the kitchen, at the table.

Just to be clear, we Masumotos have an agenda: we want more people to love peaches. This book is part of our ongoing attempt to share our love with a wider audience. We want to empower everyone to cook and eat peaches. You will find recipes, essays, snippets of stories, and kitchen tips woven throughout this book. We think of it as a literary cookbook. Our desire is that you will savor reading it in two ways. We hope that you enjoy our recipes and that they contribute to wonderful shared meals and your own creations in your home kitchen. We also hope that you enjoy parts of this book like a novel—a way to learn about farming from the voices of people who actually work the earth and to understand more about the realities we live while growing peaches. To learn more about the Masumoto Family Farm, visit www.masumoto.com. Join us in our love and lust for peaches!

I FARM STORIES • By Mas

My family taught me to have a hunger for memory. Not nostalgia for the past, but memory that's alive with a passion for excellence. My parents and grandparents instilled a desire to create a memory of something great and the passion to rediscover it each summer.

Making money was never the objective, though we acknowledged its role. Instead, our currency is about moments of meaning and a story economy where flavor has value and great peaches become gifts for the soul.

We grow stories, experiences that contribute to a collection of memories that defines us. Our wealth is measured neither in money nor land but in a portfolio of stories.

Without stories, peaches become a commodity and consumers are attracted by their cheap prices. Gone are the words that help commit experience to memory. When we lack a language of taste, we lose one of the main ingredients for creating lasting meaning. If foods are not paired with stories, no one hears the farmer's voice and the farmer is easily dismissed.

We work best as artisan farmers, exciting eaters with our spirited passion. It's okay to dream of perfection. The memory of a perfect food moment can become our greatest marketing tool. We all should hunger for memory.

CHAPTER ONE

A Peach Primer

"Start with great, end with great."

—MARCY

Peach Education / BY NIKIKO

IT IS IMPOSSIBLE to condense into a single book everything you might want to know in order to find, prepare, and enjoy a perfect peach. Nonetheless, we offer this peach primer, shorthand on some of the things we feel are most important, from anatomy to ripening to storing.

Finding the perfect peach depends on you, your tastes and preferences, and on larger structures in our food system. Although we have the privilege and responsibility of living where we grow food for ourselves and many other people, we are acutely aware of bigger forces that shape what you might encounter in the market. How you access fresh fruit, where it comes from, how it is grown, cared for (or not), handled, shipped, and unpacked all play a part in shaping what each peach can give you. In other words, finding your perfect peach is not completely in your control.

Over the course of time, peaches have evolved and mutated by chance, survival, manipulation, and "choice." People at many levels, from consumers and supermarket buyers to packers and farmers, have shifted and influenced what types of peaches are grown. The average peach today is very different from what it was a generation ago. The current trends of varieties and farming systems do not always reflect what we care most about at the Masumoto Family Farm. In many ways, our farm is an anomaly: the peaches we grow and know the best represent only a sliver of this vast species of plant. Who knows where science, technology, industry, policy, and activism will steer us next. After reading this primer—your basic peach education—you will know the fundamentals of the peach world as it is today, so that you can make the best decisions possible for you.

Here is Peaches 101. Enjoy!

THE ANATOMY OF A PEACH

Like any relationship, whether it's with yourself or another person, it's helpful and essential to know some basic anatomy for a life full of pleasure and health. In some ways, eating and feeding others is one of the most intimate exchanges among beings: we don't just consume peaches; we experience them and they become part of our bodies. Knowing where to look for that special spot on a peach will help you reach a full flavor experience. Don't remain a peach virgin!

A healthy peach is round and spherical, except for so-called doughnut, or Saturn, peaches that look like little peach tires. Connecting the "tip" end with the stem end is a seam called a suture, which divides the peach into two sections, or "cheeks." The suture is less pronounced on some varieties and more pronounced on others. When some of our old varieties, like the

Elberta, are really ripe, you can actually twist the two halves in opposite directions along the suture and break open the peach into halves, no knife required. We call the fleshy border encircling the stem end the "shoulders."

If you cut a peach in half, you can see several different layers. From the outside in, peaches have fuzz, skin or peel, flesh or meat, and finally the pit (which also has several layers inside). The color of the skin depends on a number of factors, among them the genetic disposition of the peach and how the fruit was grown.

When you live and work with peaches year after year, the anatomy becomes important in different ways. You know when packing peaches that the tip is particularly vulnerable to bruising and tearing off. You learn that the fuzz protects the fruits from infections and fungi. You appreciate the character of the suture as an aesthetic tool. We pack all of our peaches with tips up and sutures lined up in the same direction. Farming, for us, is about aesthetics in addition to (rather than in competition with) pragmatics.

YELLOW FLESH AND WHITE FLESH

In the world of peaches, two major categories exist that distinguish fruits based on the color of their flesh: yellow and white. Generally speaking, yellow-flesh peaches have more acid and thus taste tangy compared with the sweet subacid nectar of white-flesh peaches. Although there are always some glorious exceptions to this rule, when we think of white-flesh peaches, we are not overly excited. Now, this is *not* to say that white-flesh peaches are not valuable or tasty. We just want to be transparent: the Masumotos are huge fans of the acidic punch of yellow-flesh peaches. If you've never compared the two, you should try different varieties of each and follow your taste buds. Maybe you prefer one over the other, or you like them both equally. We won't hold it against you if you prefer white peaches.

It is important, however, to note that as a result of our family preference for yellow-flesh peaches (and nectarines), all of the recipes in this book were developed and tested with yellow-flesh fruits. We welcome your experimentation if you are a lover of white peaches or have access to them, but bear in mind that some of the recipes might need an extra dose of acid (try adding lemon juice) and possibly less sugar. As with all the recipes, we hope you have fun experimenting with your favored peaches!

CLING AND FREESTONE

We describe the heart of a peach—its pit—in relationship to how it connects to its surroundings. There are two designations: cling and freestone. One of our favorite nectarine varieties, the Le Grand, is the only cling stone fruit we grow on the farm. The flesh of this fruit adheres to the pit similarly to the way a mango pit is buried in and almost impossible to separate completely from its edible flesh. In other words, the fruit holds fast to the pit. Traditionally, clings were used for canning.

All of our peach varieties are freestone. Like the name, the freestone pit is unattached to the flesh of the fruit. When ripe freestone peaches are sliced in half, the pits easily come out. In the kitchen, freestone fruits are easier to work with and result in less waste. But if you are a cook working with a cling, you have a great excuse to suck the juices from the pit as a premeal sample. You wouldn't dare waste any, right?

When cooking with cling peaches (or nectarines), simply cut around the pit in a manner similar to cutting a mango. As for our Le Grand nectarines, the small inconvenience of the pit is completely worth it because flavor of the flesh is out of this world.

SEASONAL EATING: EARLY SEASON, MIDSEASON, AND LATE SEASON

In the United States, domestically grown peaches are generally available from late May through the beginning of October. Each variety ripens at a slightly different time, and every year may be slightly different depending on weather patterns. Any of the peaches you might find in the supermarket during the winter months are shipped from the Southern Hemisphere. If you're craving peaches in the off-season, think about using preserved peaches (see our recipes for frozen, dried, jammed, canned, and pickled peaches beginning on page 131) to satisfy your peach hunger. We do not recommend eating "fresh" peaches in winter, not only because they have been shipped in from so far away but also because we have always found them to be flat-out awful. Some type of preserved peach is a much more eco-minded and tasty alternative during the winter months.

The best advice on how to know when to eat which peaches is to have fun experimenting. We recommend developing a peach palate by sampling different types side by side, or by making the same recipe with different peaches throughout the harvest season. Every peach offers something slightly different. To gain an understanding of different varieties and learn about the specific varieties we raise, see page 16.

TO PEEL OR NOT TO PEEL

After years of working with peaches, we've realized that the ripe fruits of some varieties peel better than others. One variety that we grow, the Elberta, practically peels itself when ripe. You can cut into a ripe one at its tip end, loosen the skin, and pull it off with your fingers. Today Elbertas are an anomaly. We have also found that it doesn't matter what you do to peaches that are picked very green; they will not peel easily. So the first lesson in peeling is to start with ripe peaches.

Blanching is a common method of peeling ripe peaches. To do this, heat a pot of water to just below boiling. While the water is heating, prepare another large bowl of ice water. Carefully drop your peaches into the hot water for no more than one minute. Immediately remove the peaches and plunge them into the ice water. Let them cool thoroughly. The skins should slip off with a slight tug of your fingers (pictured on page 135). We have found that the blanching method does not work well for some of the more recently developed varieties. In contrast, it seems to work beautifully with heirlooms.

But the truth is, we rarely blanch our peaches simply because the thought of heating a big pot of water in our house during the summer months of triple-digit heat is less than ideal. Most of the time we just grab a good paring knife and peel by hand. It's generally easiest to start at either the shoulders or the tip, make a small slit, and then slip the blade underneath the skin. Push the blade as you turn the peach. Most of the recipes in this book assume that you have peeled the peaches, but the choice is yours.

RIPENESS

For as long as I can remember, our family has been trying to articulate how to explain when a peach is ripe. It is a nearly impossible task. To begin with, it is difficult to capture in words a sensory experience. In addition, we've been practicing finding and indulging ourselves in ripe peaches for years, and because we grow them, we almost never buy peaches from a market or store. Picking a ripe peach directly from a tree is a very different process than perusing a super-market bin. Plus, truly ripe peaches rarely arrive at most stores. Since this book is designed for the home cook, we imagine that most readers will be buying peaches, so we've written about ripeness from that perspective. It is important to understand that a ripe peach depends on context, however, so the more you learn about peaches and how you get your food, the more empowered you will be to make decisions on ripeness.

On the farm, we use particular techniques to judge when a peach is ripe. Each of the specific indicators relies on awakening the senses. Knowing when a peach is ripe is not like knowing how to multiply. It requires practice and full engagement of embodied peach perception. In our experience, for example, the aroma of a ripe peach is variable, so we look to other indicators to judge ripeness. A very ripe peach *can* have a wonderful aroma, but it's not necessarily the sole sign of maturity.

When the fruit has been already picked from the tree, we look for two big elements, background color and feel. If you study the color of a peach, you'll notice that the appearance is actually made up of tiny little circles or dots of color (similar to pointillism) on top of a background hue. A ripe yellow-flesh peach should have a yellow, amber, or golden hue behind the reddish blush. It's easiest to tell the background color by looking at the stem end. Because the sun does not directly hit the peach under the stem, most peaches are "missing" blush there, so the background color is exposed. As peaches ripen, they transform from a bright green through shades of light green, green-yellow, yellow-green, pastel yellow, and then bright yellow and even orange-yellow, gold, or amber. Inspect the color right around the stem. Does it give off light or is it dull? We often compare two peaches side by side. Where does the background color fall on the spectrum from green to gold? The ripest peaches will appear to illuminate themselves from the inside out.

To test the feel of a peach, squeeze the cheeks gently using the pads of your fingers (not the tips, which are more likely to leave a bruise or even a little slice with your fingernail). How does it feel? When we talk about the feel of a peach, we talk about a nuanced spectrum of ripeness. Over many years and four generations, we've developed the Masumoto peach vocabulary to describe different degrees of ripeness according to feel. With practice, the feel test will help you determine how ripe your peach is and what to do with it. Here's our shorthand on the stages of ripeness.

HARD. A peach that should probably not have been picked. It feels like a baseball. The skin is taut and the flesh doesn't seem to be affected at all by the pressure of your fingers. If bitten into, it will be crunchy like an apple and have no sweetness. You can try to ripen this peach, but it will most likely never reach full flavor. If this is the only peach you have to cook with, play with adding extra sugar and increasing other flavorful elements of the recipe.

FIRM. A peach that may be ready in a few days. It feels like a tennis ball and is definitely not soft, but it is not completely solid either. The flesh responds slightly to pressure, but resists significant movement or bruising. This peach needs to ripen a bit more (for ripening advice, see Storing and Ripening, opposite).

GIVE. A peach that is probably the most versatile. It is right on the edge of its most powerful flavor, so we recommend letting it sit out one or two days if it's going to be served fresh. As is, it is ideal for baking, as it will hold its shape well in the heat of the oven. When you gently squeeze a peach with give, it absorbs your subtle pressure and touch but does not leave a bruise. If you press really, really hard (which we only recommend as an experiment), your fingers will leave slight indents.

SOFT. A peach that is ready to be eaten fresh. These peaches will get bruised slightly when you squeeze them, so handle them with care. If you bruise a peach while cooking, do not fret; you can either cut out the small bruised area or just pay it no mind. Soft peaches are wonderful gifts. It is important to note that there is a fine line between the feel of a soft peach and a mealy peach, but they are not the same (see our discussion of mealy, opposite).

GUSHY OR GUSHER. A peach that you want to eat right now over the kitchen sink. It is over-ripe and most likely bruised already. It will feel heavy with juice and sugar and is perfect for jam or purees. These are the ones we fight over on the farm. Most consumers have probably never seen a gusher because these peaches rarely make it through industrial packing systems. Again, like the soft peach, this should not be confused with mealy.

BRUISE. An area on a peach that is flattened or indented. When you cut into the area of a bruise, you will note that the flesh is slightly discolored and looks light brown. This is caused either by slight to moderate pressure against a ripe area or occasionally by incredible force on a hard or firm peach. One of our lessons is not to be afraid of bruises. Most often they can help indicate a ripe piece of fruit. We simply cut out the discolored part when we're cooking. Why throw out the baby with the bath water? Remember, gushers are often bruised and also the most flavorful.

MEALY. One of the most frustrating states of a peach. The texture of a mealy peach is soft but also grainy because the cell structure of the flesh has begun to break down. A mealy peach is way past its prime or was picked while it was still green, then refrigerated and brought out to room temperature again. When an immature peach is picked and refrigerated, it will never ripen correctly. It will only get mealy.

DEHYDRATED. If kept a very long time, any peach, both the immature ones and the ripe ones, will dehydrate. The skin will look wrinkly and the peach will feel spongy. When cut into, it will not be juicy. Peaches that are picked immature and remain in refrigeration too long are the most prone to dehydration.

STORING AND RIPENING

Once you have picked up your peaches (hopefully somewhere in the firm to gushy range), you can manage the ripeness by storing them in different ways. If the peaches were picked close to their peak of ripeness, you actually have quite a bit of power over them. Some varieties continue to ripen better than others. We've noticed that our older varieties, such as the Elberta and Sun Crest, ripen much better off the tree than newer varieties.

Once you have your peaches at home, sort them by ripeness. Peaches are ideally stored resting on their shoulders and not touching one another. If you have peaches that you would like to ripen further, leave them out at room temperature in a dry area. You can even leave them outside or near a window to get direct sunlight (but do not let them bake in the hot sun). Check them daily, and when they are ready, either use them or store them in the refrigerator.

Peaches that were picked very green will not ripen, even if left out at room temperature. Green-hard peaches that have been refrigerated will go from green to mealy when left out. Thus, once again, it is best to purchase peaches that are the closest to their peak.

Once you put peaches in refrigeration (the temperature of a household refrigerator is great), you will dramatically stop the ripening process. Very ripe peaches (like gushers) will keep in the refrigerator for days at a time before they breakdown too much. Monitor them daily and be wary of signs of dehydration.

PEACH SIGNATURE

Much like when human skin is exposed to sunlight, our peaches change color depending on the angle of the sun when it kisses their cheeks and what might be providing shade. One of our favorite things to do is to find a peach that has been hanging with a leaf over its sunny side. Lifting the leaf will reveal what my dad calls the "peach leaf signature." Underneath the leaf is a bright yellow area that was shaded from the sun's rays, outlined by beautiful blush where the sun touched the peach directly around the leaf.

READY TO PERFORM

After reading this primer, we hope you feel peach empowered! None of the information here reflects hard-and-fast rules because so much of the lived experience of cooking with and eating peaches cannot be captured on the page. Cooking requires impromptu adjustments, learning by doing, experimentation, and risk taking. In this way, we invite you to think of our recipes like they are the script of a great peach play. They are maps, guidelines, and stage directions open to interpretation and waiting to come alive. We have written each of them with much care, but only with your help, the cook and eater, can these dishes be enjoyed. The magic is born when the words are transformed in and through bodies and shared with an audience of eaters. We invite you to experience your perfect peach by interpreting our recipes with your own flair and passion. Take all the rehearsal time you want. The kitchen is your stage, and you are its star. Start with a great peach and know that our gratitude and applause are imminent.

LESSONS I HAVE LEARNED COOKING WITH PEACHES • By Marcy

When I first came to the farm, I tried to save every peach that dropped in the orchard, and every one that was not fit for packing and selling commercially. Finally, after years of painstaking cooking and preserving, I realized that there was no way I could save all the orphaned or special-needs peaches from our twenty-five acres of orchards! Now, after thirty years of working with peaches in this farmhouse kitchen, here are ten lessons to guide you as you work and cook with peaches.

1. Not every peach you touch is going to be fantastic—flavorful and perfect for the use you have in mind. It helps if you get to know your peaches, where they are from, when they were picked, how they were handled, and the attributes of those you have in hand, to determine the best use of that peach.

2. If you start with a great peach, you can end with a great-tasting dish. If you start with a bad peach (such as one that was picked green or has been in cold storage for weeks or months), you will end up with a bad-tasting dish. Flavor should trump aesthetics. The less you do to a good-tasting peach, the better!

3. The more you work with a particular peach variety, the better you will know its best uses and what adjustments you need to make to recipes. Always taste one of your peaches before starting a recipe to know what kind of modifications, if any, you need to make to the directions.

4. Some peaches peel easier than others. Typically, older varieties and riper peaches will peel easier than newer varieties and less-ripe fruit.

5. Some peaches are sweeter than others, some more tart. Where your peaches fall on the sweet-tart spectrum will dictate how much sweetener (sugar, honey, other) and/or acid (lemon juice, lime juice, other) you will need to add to a recipe.

6. Some peaches are juicier than others. The degree of juiciness will determine how much

(continued)

thickener (flour, cornstarch, tapioca, other) you will need to add to your baked goods (pie, cobbler, crisp, *crostata*, galette, or other treat).

7. When uncooked peach flesh is exposed to air, it oxidizes and turns brown. This is easily avoided by coating the surface of the fruit with lemon juice or another acidic element or with a commercial ascorbic acid product such as Fruit Fresh. You can also wait until the last minute to cut and serve peaches to minimize "air time." Your hands will also turn brown if you have lots of peach juice on your skin and under your nails from peeling and cutting peaches. To avoid this, rinse your peach-drenched hands, including under your nails, with lemon juice.

8. If you talk to a farmer, a produce manager, or an old-timer with a backyard orchard, you may be able to find good-tasting older peach varieties that remind you of the ones you ate with your grandmother or grandfather when you were a kid or that you picked ripe from the tree way back when.

9. If you are buying fresh peaches in the United States between October and April, chances are they have traveled a long distance (such as from the Southern Hemisphere), have been refrigerated for a long time (weeks or months), and are not as good as what you might get from the freezer, a jar, or a package.

10. Yes, you can eat too many peaches at one time, which will likely lead to a stomach ache! Every summer, we Masumotos find that we need to lay off peaches for a few days several times during the harvest to give our digestive tracts a rest. I do not recommend eating more than two or three peaches a day!

Peach Varieties: Our (Magnificent?) Seven
/ BY MAS

Peaches often remain nameless in the market. It's not that they are humble and reserved. If ripe and ready, they can reach out with their glow and aroma, a siren for the fruit lover.

One reason peaches are not often identified by variety name in stores is because there are so many different varieties. Forty years ago, in the late 1970s, California alone grew about forty major varieties that produced twelve million boxes or 270 million pounds for the fresh market (peaches destined for canning are counted separately by the industry). This does not include the numerous exclusive varieties with small production totals that go uncounted by the industry. By 2008, there were over one hundred major varieties just in California that produced over twenty-four million boxes; almost all of the ones that were on the 1970 list, like the varieties we grow on our farm, were no longer counted because they were produced in small volumes. Add in South Carolina and Georgia with their assorted varieties, along with what is grown in the dozens of other peach-producing states and regions, and there are probably thousands of varieties from which to choose. In other words, a huge volume of peaches is constantly moving in and out of the many markets. No single variety dominates the market, and naming the "best" peaches poses a challenge.

I like to think the lack of name branding has to do with character: peaches are as varied as the people who grow them. The Masumoto Sun Crest peach will be different from the same peach variety grown by another farmer north or south of us. Our earliest variety, Spring Lady, which is harvested in May, is very different from our late-arriving August Elberta. Even within a single variety's harvest window, the first round of picking the fruit is much different from the final round ten days later. Include the fact that one year may be different from another due to weather, and the name attached to a peach may not mean much. Shopping by variety alone may not always make sense.

The exception to this may be farmers' markets and a few select stores, but even the peaches found in those venues will have character issues, and variation will remain the rule. Also complicating selection is the fact that the typical peach is only ripe and harvested over a ten- to fourteen-day period. By the time you go back to the store, there's a good chance your peach will have been replaced by the next ripening variety.

So how do you tell one variety from another? We suggest that you find the people and places that offer great peaches for your needs (based on flavor, availability, convenience, seasonality, and price) and you fall in love with them.

By exploring the seven different peach varieties we grow on our farm, you might also get insight and the backstory about the variation among varieties. The differences are distinct. Our peaches remain as varied as latitudes and attitudes. They work for us but not for necessarily for everyone—like life and people.

We call them our magnificent seven, not because they're always gloriously the same but because they are magnificently varied.

SPRING LADY

Our earliest peach, harvested the fourth week of May. Planted in 1985, the year Nikiko was born. A newer variety when first introduced in the 1980s. Today is considered out-of-date.

The flavor of this peach has evolved on the farm. First, it was young and sharp. Then through the adolescent teen years (thirteen to nineteen years old), the taste was good but not mature—like it stayed out too late at night. But near year twenty, the flavor changed and finally matured, as if the peach moved out of the house, got educated, found a job, and settled down.

(The profits from Spring Lady went straight into Nikiko's college fund. It was a good thing she went to public UC Berkeley and not a private college.)

Flavors can be outstanding, but the fruit may be difficult to peel. We planted this variety originally to take advantage of good early-market prices. But now even earlier domestic varieties are hitting the marketplace. Can you believe California-grown peaches in April?

PHRASE THAT BEST DESCRIBES: Patient parents sometimes rewarded.

JUNE CREST

Ripens early June. Planted in the 1990s because we believed in family genes (it's a cousin to the Sun Crest). Industry dislike: the big suture. (Newer varieties bred out this seeming defect, however, though the size of the suture never bothered our family. Flavor trumps shape in peaches and people). Concern: Although this is an exceptional and versatile peach, it is not yet an OMG experience. Question: Patience required? It needs a few more years to settle down and grow deep roots in our soil.

PHRASE THAT BEST DESCRIBES: Very good but waiting for maturity.

GOLD DUST

Ripens mid-June. An old heirloom, first propagated in 1940s, Gold Dust is the mother (or father) of Sun Crest. Outstanding flavor, but the fruit size is a little small by today's standards (a fruit 2⅝ inches in diameter can be worthless compared to a fruit 3 inches in diameter—size does matter). Flavor much like a buttery apricot. Makes a golden jam (page 137). Significance: We loved the idea of going backward, finding the parent of something great.

SADDEST MOMENT: One year, we left too many fruits on the trees and had to drop 70 percent of the crop to the ground because no one wanted small fruit.

PHRASE THAT BEST DESCRIBES: The real gold rush for the Masumoto Family Farm.

FLAVOR CREST

Ripens end of June, just before Sun Crest. Pedigree: A cousin of the Sun Crest—which dreams of being as good as its stellar kin—the Flavor Crest was introduced to farmers in 1960s, became a hit, and is still produced in large quantities today. We planted it in our orchard in the 1990s. This is the peach you take home to meet your parents: solid, sweet, understanding, outstanding flavor, blush color. Fantastic for Caprese with Peaches (page 54) or spinach salad (page 68).

HAPPIEST MOMENT: Our Flavor Crest was served at one of the nation's best restaurants in New York.

SADDEST MOMENT: Same as above, because we worried that achieving the goal of being served at one of the country's finest restaurants might mean our farm had peaked, a response that demonstrates either our humility or eternal lack of confidence.

PHRASE THAT BEST DESCRIBES: Good family genes.

ELEGANT LADY

Ripens mid-July. Yes, this is the name of a peach—probably named by a male, no? When we planted the Elegant Lady in 1980, it was considered a "modern" peach. Nice sharp peach taste and fits the modern-produce specifications: good size, stores well, and good looking. Why did we plant it? Insurance, in case our "unattractive but good" theory of peaches ran into a wall.

PHRASE THAT BEST DESCRIBES: This peach will make money.

SUN CREST

Midseason peach, ripens on our farm about the Fourth of July. We planted our Sun Crest orchard in 1968, so it is now our old-growth forest by peach standards (the industry usually keeps a peach for ten to fifteen years before discarding the old for something new). A few years ago, we held a fortieth birthday party for this peach and invited outstanding chefs to toast and cook for guests. It was a fantastic affair!

The Sun Crest has OMG flavor, grows to a huge size, and boasts a flaming amber blush. The United States Department of Agriculture developed the Sun Crest sixty years ago, blending the best of very old heirlooms with the goal of creating a fruit that could sell in the modern market-place. It was an era when government worked for the common good, and we paid no royalties to a private nursery for our trees. Today, almost all new stone-fruit varieties are developed by private nurseries that patent them and collect royalties from the farmers who plant them.

This peach dreamed of becoming the industry darling and was widely planted in California, then it learned the cruel lesson of the aging movie star: looks matter. But the earned income from this peach orchard paid for my college education (again, like Nikiko, I went to a public, not a private, college). Weakness: doesn't always remain firm when heated (cooking, baking, canning) but the taste is still fantastic. A family favorite, this peach loves to be eaten fresh or frozen.

PHRASE THAT BEST DESCRIBES: Inspiration for my book, *Epitaph for a Peach*.

ELBERTA

Ripens early August. This is the mother of all peaches, at least by reputation. Ask someone older than sixty and he or she might sigh when the name Elberta is mentioned, renewing fond memories. Once the nation's most popular peach. Can be picked green and still ripen. Originally it was sold as a "wrap," that is, tissue-thin paper was wrapped around each peach before it was placed in the packing box.

This is the classic peach for canning. Amazing fruit for cooking or baking, and keeps its shape and color no matter how it is prepared. On our farm, we describe it as "a peach that gets even better when you add heat." Indeed, it makes the average cook look better because it takes to heat so well. Problem: On our farm, Elbertas can be very delicate when ripe. Staring at them on the tree may result in bruises (a favorite saying of ours and a slight exaggeration). A veteran farmer also once quipped that when picked golden ripe, this peach will bruise on the way from the tree to the kitchen. The Elberta was the inspiration for our farm's adopt-a-tree program: people saved our Elbertas by adopting a tree and coming to the farm to harvest their peach babies. We are now working with master brewers who are creating a sour fruit ale called Lambic using our Elbertas, along with a few other of our peach and nectarine varieties.

There are dozens of Elberta varieties. Peaches often grow "sports," a type of mutation that sometimes captures the best of the original tree with something new. Other farmers may grow a firmer Elberta or one that can be picked green and shipped. Our Elberta happens to be a very demanding one, perhaps mirroring the farmer.

PHRASE THAT BEST DESCRIBES: Magical peach that makes us appreciate old things.

TEN STUPID MISTAKES I HAVE MADE ON THE FARM • By Mas

Admitting errors can make you question your abilities, challenge your confidence, and hurt your business, yet it also makes your work more human. We farmers work intimately with both nature and human nature, ensuring that our life's calling is filled with lessons.

1. Believing trees would tell me if they're hungry or thirsty. Usually by the time they show symptoms, it's too late. They'll abort their crop when threatened.
2. Ignoring my physical health. I had a small hernia in my late twenties, and believing I was invincible, I waited until I was in my fifties to have it fixed. I suffered for decades and even now the fix, with scar tissue replacing smooth muscles, isn't complete.
3. Working with denial. Very wet springs breed diseases like brown rot on peaches. But pathogens are not visible, so I fool myself into thinking they're not affecting me, until the rot arrives just at harvest, when the fungi or bacteria thrive on sugars. Then the invisible abruptly become visible.
4. Thinking too much when planting wildflowers on the farm. They're beautiful, early to bloom in the spring, and can find niches to

(continued)

grow in and thrive. But if you planted them, can they still be wildflowers?

5. Trusting stickers. Years ago, some large grocery stores demanded we sticker our peaches. We had to apply on each peach one of those little labels with a price look-up code. But our heirloom peaches often had lots of fuzz, and early on, the food-grade adhesives were not good. I remember driving down the road with a truckload of peach boxes and watching thousands of stickers flying off in the wind. Cars behind me were weaving, trying to dodge the Masumoto Family Farm stickers so that they wouldn't adhere to their windshields.

6. Believing that water could flow uphill. Against all logic, when I irrigated the highest ground on our farm, I wanted to believe that the water would flow uphill. Those trees always suffered from thirst. That's why no other farmers planted crops on the high ground. They knew the land was worthless for planting, so they build farmhouses there instead. That's where our home sits, with a grand view, too.

7. Thinking I'm smarter than animals. Farm dogs know better than to work in 110°F heat. Once during a heat wave, I wanted to finish disking an orchard, pulling a set of steel blades through the earth behind a tractor to knock down weeds and turn the soil. I sat on the tractor for hours before coming home ill from heat exhaustion. Our dogs, resting coolly under the shade of a tree, just looked at me and shook their heads.

8. Getting the tractor stuck in the mud at the same spot in the orchard. That patch of earth must be haunted, ambushing me over and over! Actually, in that spot, there was a leaky underground cement irrigation pipe that slowly seeped water. Also, once you have compacted the earth with spinning tires sinking deeper and deeper, the sandy loam does form a "pan" of compressed soil particles that do not drain well. Fool me once or twice . . . but what does it mean when I'm fooled a dozen times?

9. Adding up losses in the middle of a harvest when we're getting lousy prices for our peaches. During such a crisis, you have two choices. If it is irreparably dismal, you stop picking and leave the fruit to fall on the ground. This has happened only rarely. Most of the time you engage plan B: you work through it, trying to recover as many of your costs as possible. You're bleeding, but do you really need to know how badly? Would it change anything?

10. Failing to follow a straight line. In 1968, when I was a kid, I helped my father plant our Sun Crest orchard, a peach with amazing taste. His rows were straight; he took his time. My rows were a little crooked, but it didn't matter to an impatient teenager. Decades later, I still have to swerve around the trees that are not lined up correctly and thus lean too far to one side. And I always imagine my father watching me.

CHAPTER TWO

Thirst and Sweat
BEVERAGES and STORIES ABOUT WORK

"The first taste of a peach announces summer has arrived."

—MAS

AGUA de DURAZNO

I first learned to make *agua fresca* from new friends while living in Oaxaca, Mexico. I was twenty and a foreign-exchange student on my first extended trip outside of the United States. I was very green. I spent time in two pueblos, Santa Ana del Valle and San Juan Mixtepec. Both are places of lively linguistic movement and flow: in Santa Ana, both Zapoteco and Spanish are spoken, and in San Juan, Mixteco and Spanish. My Spanish was nascent and I knew nothing of Mixteco or Zapoteco. Food was one of the strongest vehicles by which I could participate in daily exchanges of meaning. I observed, made a fool of myself, tasted everything that was shared, and tried to dance through the steps of dialogue, ignorance, and difference toward understanding. Missteps were inevitable, like the night I stupidly thought I ordered duck (*pato*) from a street vendor and got a plate of pigs' feet (*patas*).

Agua fresca was one of the recipes I learned from oral instructions, like "add some sugar and some water." It calls for engaged cooking, so I have never seen anyone make it from a written recipe. And no two batches are the same. Every cook I encountered adjusted the ratio of water and sugar depending on the fruit. My recipe is meant as a loose guideline, an archive of the food knowledge generously shared with me. It should be served ice-cold to shake off a day of heat. I love *agua fresca* because it is flexible and invigorating and it takes me back to the homes of my friends in Oaxaca who taught me the most: Eva in San Juan Mixtepec, and José in Santa Ana del Valle.

Nikiko

2   gushy peaches, peeled, pitted, and quartered

1/4   to 1/3 cup turbinado sugar

4   to 6 cups water
    Squeeze of fresh lime juice
    Ice cubes, for serving

4   to 6 mint sprigs, for garnish
    (optional)

Place the peaches, sugar, and water in a blender and process until the sugar has dissolved and the peaches are liquefied. Add the lime juice and process briefly to mix. Serve in tall glasses over ice. Garnish with the mint sprigs.

Sweat / BY MAS

I'M NOT SURE you understand sweat.

Out on the farm, I've tasted sweat, a salty, tangy flavor as it drips down my temples, beads on my upper lip, and slips across my cheeks.

Farmwork makes me sweat. It first appears on my chest, seeping through my pores, subtle and silent, unannounced on bare skin. A damp chill tickles my body, yet sends me a simple message: *hot.* I can feel my T-shirt and work shirt stick to my flesh, cling to my body. I grow conscious of my heavy breathing. I can feel moisture in my hair. My forehead beads. I wipe away the perspiration, blinking to keep it out of my eyes.

I'm losing liquids. I can't go forever. I have to stop sometime. Sweat reminds me of limits. Sweat defines the character of our farm. I think of sweat as clean and honest.

When I sweat, T-shirt and work shirt are the first articles of clothing soaked, followed by hat and gloves, not to mention underwear and socks. On a few scorching days, even my leather belt is stained. The only parts of my clothes that are never soaked with my sweat are the belt loops on my pants.

Summer work in 100°F heat. Hellishly hot. I sweat just by walking outside. Ubiquitous heat, like a furnace with no escape exit door. Fool to be out in this kind of heat. But grapes and peaches demand it, and if I'm thirsty, so are they.

The work and heat beat me up. I lean over, panting. Take short breaths, save energy, feel the heart race and veins and arteries pulsate. I want to quit, not worth it, sweating is cutting years off my life. A drip off my chin, my nose, draining life away.

But farmwork needs to be done. Sagging branches need staking before snapping. Dead limbs must be dragged away like corpses. Weeds grow wild, sapping moisture. And peaches cry out, grapes beg for water. Hard work, hard sweat.

Is this what I must do to keep farming? Work more. Work faster. The struggling craftsman, the starving artist.

An old farmer told me sweating will harden you. I thought he meant the tough lessons of life. Now I know better. Hard sweat drains me of youth. I feel old, years lost to the hard, physical work of farming. I've changed from a young farmer to an old one with nothing in between. Sacrifice years for a juicy peach or sweet raisin. Work beats me again and again. Start out young, and after just a few years of sweat, you discover you're old.

I stagger home and collapse on the farmhouse porch. My children see me. They worry. Something wrong. "You okay, Dad?"

My eyes stay shut. I shake my head. "This farm's gonna kill me."

They stand silently. They know I'm telling the truth.

GINGER-PEACH SODA

SERVES 4 TO 6

On triple-digit summer days when I have expelled more sweat from my body than I think is possible, replenishing fluids is part of my job. (We can't forget that the health of farmers and farmworkers is a key part of sustainable agriculture.) Although I prefer water, sometimes its zero-calorie refreshment is not quite enough. When I need some sweetness and effervescence, I turn to this homemade soda recipe. It is healthier than commercial soda (economically, environmentally, and biologically) and is a nice treat that reenergizes me for more work.

Nikiko

GINGER SIMPLE SYRUP

1   cup water

1   cup sugar

1   (2-inch) piece fresh ginger, the thickness of a thumb, peeled and minced

1   soft to gushy peach, halved, pitted, and thinly sliced

    Ice cubes, for serving

    Soda water, to fill

    Fresh mint leaves, for garnish (optional)

To make the syrup, in a saucepan, combine the water, sugar, and ginger over medium-low heat and stir until the sugar has dissolved. Remove from the heat, cover, and steep at room temperature for about 30 minutes.

Pour the syrup through a fine-mesh sieve to remove the ginger, pressing all the flavor out of the ginger with the back of a spoon against the sieve. Transfer to a jar or other storage container, cover, and refrigerate until well chilled.

Evenly distribute the peach slices among the glasses. Carefully smash the peaches with the end of a wooden spoon to release their juice. Pour about 2 tablespoons chilled syrup over the peaches in each glass. (The remaining syrup can be stored in the refrigerator for up to 2 weeks.) Add ice cubes and then top off each glass with soda water. Mix each drink with a straw or spoon to distribute the syrup, peach juices, and peach bits evenly. Float a few mint leaves on each serving, then serve immediately (especially on really hot days).

PEACH QUENCHER

Summer afternoons in the Fresno area can be incredibly hot—so hot that after working outside your body heats up, turns red, starts sweating, and you don't think you can possibly cool down. On days like those, especially when coming in from a day of packing fruit, we enjoy this simple thirst quencher.

Marcy

2	or 3 gushy peaches, peeled, pitted, and quartered
³/4	cup pineapple juice
1/2	cup frozen lemonade concentrate, partially thawed
1	to 1¹/2 cups crushed ice or ice cubes
1¹/2	cups soda water (also known as club soda)
4	mint sprigs or thin peach slices, for garnish

Put the peaches in a blender and process to yield 2 cups puree. Add the pineapple juice, lemonade concentrate, and 1 cup ice and process until the mixture is slushy, adding more ice as needed to get a good consistency. Stir in the soda water.

Pour into chilled tall glasses and garnish each serving with a mint sprig.

Cook's Note: You may also use partially thawed Frozen Peaches (page 148) or Peach Puree (page 49) for this drink. If you don't have lemonade concentrate, substitute 4 tablespoons freshly squeezed lemon juice and 2 tablespoons sugar.

PEACH-MINT LASSI

Every summer we drop off peaches on our neighbors' front steps or ask them to stop by for a bucket of our best gushers. We participate in an unspoken "gift economy," as my dad calls it. In return, we have received things like homemade tamales, spring rolls, pomegranate jelly, and dolmas. These exchanges help to explain the *terroir* of the Central Valley, not only by its climactic and topographical growing conditions but also by the human geography of food production. For centuries in California, immigrants have and continue to shape our food system fundamentally. I am thankful for the generosity of my neighbors and our workers, and the food traditions we bring and teach one another. *Lassi* is a drink that ties the Central Valley to South Asia. There are infinite versions, some savory and some sweet. My humble interpretation is inspired by mango *lassi*, with peaches replacing the mango and the addition of some mint from our garden. Nectarines would also make a delicious version. I hope the policies that govern our borders will one day mirror the pleasures of sharing foods across culture, place, and heritage. Without our neighbors, without immigrants, our recipes, our farm, and our valley could not survive.

Nikiko

1 soft or gushy large peach, peeled, pitted, and quartered

5 ice cubes

1 cup plain or flavored yogurt

¼ cup water

5 or 6 fresh mint leaves

1 to 2 tablespoons sugar, or 1½ teaspoons to 1 tablespoon honey

1 or 2 mint sprigs, for garnish (optional)

Combine the peach, ice cubes, yogurt, water, mint leaves, and 1 tablespoon sugar in a blender and process until smooth and the mint leaves are evenly distributed in the form of tiny green confetti. Taste and adjust with more sugar if needed.

Pour into 1 or 2 glasses and float a mint sprig on top.

How to Prune and Thin a Tree / BY MAS

PEACH TREES want to be pruned. They bear fruit on one-year-old wood, in other words, only the new green shoots will have fruit the following year. Peaches want to become trees not bushes; the proper structure has an open center and long "hangers" (that's what we call the new branches). The fruit that gets the most sunlight will grow the best and taste the best. Peaches worship the sun, and so should you.

That's why the overall shape of a peach tree is crucial: it needs to allow as much sunlight as possible to penetrate the canopy. All of our trees are goblet shaped, with the major limbs trained upward and bent out from the trunk, forming a gentle curve. The scaffolds do not grow overly upright and straight, like a champagne glass. The center must be open to allow the tree to gather in the natural light of spring and summer. But the tree must not be so wide at the top that it resembles a martini glass. Instead imagine the shape of a white-wine glass, relatively wide at the top, gradually bending inward at the bottom, with no radical or abrupt angles—a relaxed contour allowing maximum light and air.

It helps to know your adult beverages when you prune. And afterward, too, with glass in hand as you sit back to admire your sculpture of branches and light.

A typical peach tree may have thousands of blossoms and eventually puny fruit. Without "thinning," or knocking off, part of the crop, the peaches will end up as tiny, golf-ball-size fruits, more pit than meat and not very appetizing.

A healthy full-grown peach tree may have three thousand to five thousand thumb-size green fruits in April. We then "thin," knocking off as much as 80 to 90 percent of the crop to the ground. The earth is blanketed with a layer of aborted fruit. It's a necessary step, otherwise the fruits will be very, very small and worthless—little peach to eat. We try to leave only four hundred to seven hundred fruits on each tree for harvest. Given a choice, a peach tree wants a smaller crop. Relieved of the stress and constraint, they will produce much larger, juicer peaches and stay healthy.

But it's hard not to stare at all the fruit on the ground at this time of the year. My father told me not to look down but to keep my head up and eyes focused on the real prize: the fruit we keep and sustain that will now thrive.

PEACH-ROSEMARY BELLINI

I am a lazy gardener. On the farm, we have two gardens, a year-round herb patch and a small summer vegetable plot. But my laziness is not my fault. It is the fault of one plant, rosemary. Rosemary is one of the easiest things to grow in our climate (and in other areas with good drainage, I'm told) and ours thrives: it always looks happy and wild. Plus, it doesn't need me very much. As a result, I don't feel guilty about neglecting it and my laziness is validated. I created this recipe to add the earthy aroma of rosemary and a humble twist to this classic, elegant peach beverage. I realize that not all plants need us very much to be delicious.

Nikiko

ROSEMARY SIMPLE SYRUP

1/2 cup water

1/4 cup sugar

1 (2 1/2-inch) rosemary sprig

2 gushy peaches, peeled, pitted, and quartered

1 (750-ml) bottle Prosecco, chilled

To make the syrup, in a saucepan, combine the water and sugar over medium-low heat and stir until the sugar has dissolved. Remove from the heat, add the rosemary, cover, and steep at room temperature for about 30 minutes.

Lift out and discard the rosemary. Transfer the syrup to a jar or other storage container, cover, and refrigerate until well chilled. (Syrup will keep in refrigerator for up to 2 weeks.)

Using a mortar and pestle, smash the peach to a pulpy consistency. Press the peach pulp through a fine-mesh sieve with the back of a spoon and collect only its juice in a small bowl.

To make each drink, combine 1 tablespoon peach juice and 1 tablespoon simple syrup in a champagne glass. Top off each glass with about 1/2 cup Prosecco. Serve immediately.

SUMMER SANGRIA

When peaches are in season, we use them every way we can. The beauty of sangria is that if you have peaches, you can use them in several forms—slices, nectar, brandy—or not! You do not need to start with expensive wine. You just want something that will provide a solid base for the combination of flavors. I personally like a drier white like a Sauvignon Blanc for this recipe. The secret to good sangria is to make it in the morning or the day before, so that the fruit has enough time to soak and meld with the other flavors. This adult beverage is a great way to enjoy the best of summer with family or friends, especially as the sun sets.

Marcy

½ orange, sliced

½ lemon, sliced

1 lime, sliced

Juice of ½ orange

Juice of ½ lemon

1 (750-ml) bottle white wine (such as Sauvignon Blanc, Riesling, Pinot Grigio, or Chardonnay)

½ cup simple syrup or peach nectar (see page 36)

¼ cup brandy or Peach-Infused Brandy (page 39)

1 peach with give, halved, pitted, and thinly sliced

½ cup berries (such as raspberries, boysenberries, or sliced strawberries)

Place the orange, lemon, and lime slices in the bottom of a large pitcher and mash gently with a long wooden spoon to release some of the juice. Add the orange and lemon juices, wine, simple syrup, and brandy and stir gently to mix. Add the peach slices and berries. Cover and refrigerate for up to 1 day so flavors meld.

Pour into tall glasses or wineglasses, spooning the fruit into the glasses, and serve.

To make simple syrup, combine 1 cup each water and sugar in a saucepan and heat over medium-low heat, stirring until the sugar has dissolved. Remove from the heat and let cool. Transfer to a jar or other container, cover, and refrigerate to use in beverages or to make peach nectar. You should have 1½ cups of syrup. It will keep for about two weeks in an airtight container in the refrigerator.

To make peach nectar, add 1 large gushy peach, peeled, pitted, and sliced or pureed, to the simple syrup while the syrup is still warm enough to heat the peaches through. Let cool completely, then transfer the mixture to a jar, cover, and refrigerate for at least 1 day or up to 2 weeks. Strain through a fine-mesh sieve before using. Alternatively, use the syrup from Canned Peaches (page 134) in place of peach nectar.

Ghosts of Farmworkers / BY MAS

THE GHOSTS OF FARMWORKERS haunt my fields. I see them in the fading light at dusk, trudging homeward after a long, sweaty workday. I also feel them on cold, bitter foggy mornings, huddled around a makeshift fire of burning stumps and branches, trying to warm stiff hands before attacking another row that needs pruning. I hear their whispers, reminding me of the hours of labor needed to grow a harvest, the hands that touch and nurture peaches as they evolve from blossoms to tiny green fruit and eventually lush, bulbous, fat, and juicy treasures.

A great peach only comes from the many hands of workers. They're invisible, forgotten, alone, even as they methodically march through our fields. Often only the farmer knows of them, haunted by their presence. Without these unseen hands, we would not have peaches.

My grandparents and parents were farmworkers, immigrants to a foreign land with a history of exploiting cheap laborers and then casting them aside and importing another source of strong backs and fast hands. Our family lost everything with the brutal uprooting of World War II relocation and the forced removal of all Japanese Americans from the Pacific coast because they looked like the enemy. The government believed the invisible were justified causalities of the war.

Because of our history, my father and I often worked side by side with laborers, sharing the sweat yet acutely aware of our class differences. I the farmer, they the farmworkers. Today, those who work the land are more respected, but that doesn't always translate into higher income and wages. We're all caught in a vicious economic system of inexpensive food, consumers often paying the least they can, and farmers trying to compete in a system that breaks relationships down into monetary transactions.

Each year, farmers strive to work more efficiently and productively; they push to exploit every opportunity, sometimes driving themselves, their families, and the workers too hard and long. The landscape is then filled with more and more ghosts: farmers who grew depressed from the never-ending pressures of the physical work and farmworkers who were broken from the long brutal hours in the fields. Perhaps they all should concede and accept a system of cheap wages for cheap food.

Yet in the fields, the work continues, people labor in silence, rarely asking for more, seemingly content. Of course, they're invisible.

The workers have left their mark on our trees and vines. We have ninety-year-old grapevines that bear the signs of skillful pruning by decades of workers. My grandparents may have worked these vines as common laborers, the white farmer hiring work crews of Japanese Americans.

Now I'm the farmer and live with this legacy and stain. I hope things are changing. Organic farming and a new interest in food has resulted in better prices and more scrutiny. Workers may come out of the shadows, light shined on their faces. I dream of fair-trade policies with progressive peaches and radical raisins. Skeptics of my farming scoff at my ideas. Some politicians and public policy advocates demand change immediately. But the system is slow to adjust and adapt. I think critics haven't worked around the invisible lately.

Imagine sharing a great meal with ghosts of farmworkers. Ghosts become part of the conversation; their stories belong alongside great chefs and cooks. The culinary arts can only truly evolve when all the hands of the workers are respected. All the arts must have less ego, be less self-centered, be more communal in nature. That's not how the arts are typically portrayed today, and that's why the culinary arts can be different: more respect-ful, engaging on a new level that transcends the visual or aural arts. Imagine tasting and feeling art and at the same time connecting with the story behind the foods. The potential excites: the new currency of good food may be hope and change.

The ghosts stay with me in the fields. Perhaps my contribution is to tell the story of the invisible. I know that one day I too will become a ghost.

PEACH-INFUSED BRANDY

When I was a kid, my mom made brandied fruits and I always hated them! The fermented fruit was just too strong for my young taste buds. Now that I'm an adult (and have adult children), I find that I much prefer the fruit-infused liquor over the fermented fruit itself. This recipe is about as easy as could be and is a real winner if you enjoy fruit-flavored spirits. You can use vodka or gin as a substitute for the brandy, if you like, though I have always preferred brandy.

Marcy

1 cup peeled and sliced or diced very ripe soft or gushy peaches, including juices

3 cups brandy

Drop the peach pieces into a sterilized 1-quart jar. Pour in the brandy, filling the jar to within about 1/2 inch of the rim. Screw on the clean lid and place the jar in the back of the refrigerator. Shake the jar every few days to mix up the fruit and expose it to the brandy.

After 2 weeks, taste the liquid to see if it has as much peach flavor as you like. If not, return it to the refrigerator for another week or two. About 4 weeks should be ample time for the transfer of flavor. When you think the brandy has the level of peachiness you want, pour the mixture through a fine-mesh sieve or a coffee-filter-lined funnel to remove the little peach bits, then transfer the liquid to another sterilized jar. Cover and store in the refrigerator or a dark cabinet until needed. It will keep indefinitely, but I recommend drinking it by the time peaches are available the next year.

PEACH LIQUEUR I

This is a sweet version of Peach-Infused Brandy and may be enjoyed as an after-dinner drink.

Marcy

1 cup peeled and sliced or diced very ripe soft or gushy peaches, including juices

½ cup sugar

3 cups of your favorite brandy, vodka, or gin

Follow the directions for Peach-Infused Brandy (page 39), adding the sugar with the peaches. Let the sugar granules dissolve before pouring the brandy into the jar, then proceed as directed.

PEACH LIQUEUR II

Here's another way to make a sweet peach-infused liqueur from your homemade peach brandy to enjoy with family and friends.

Marcy

¾ cup Peach-Infused Brandy (page 39)

¼ cup simple syrup (page 36)

Combine the brandy and syrup in a jar, mix well, cover, and refrigerate until well chilled. Serve in your favorite cordial glasses.

PEACH MARGARITA

SERVES 4

Sometimes, especially if things go wrong, we need a drink—an adult beverage. After the day's work is done, there's nothing like sipping icy margaritas as we sit on our farmhouse porch to rest and regroup. If you are a margarita fan, you know that the type of tequila used influences the flavor of the drink, so select your favorite tequila for this recipe. For a different effect, I sometimes coat the rim of the glass with fine sugar flavored with grated lemon and/ or lime zest, but the salt-rimmed glasses make it a more classic drink. This recipe works best when all the ingredients and the glasses are chilled.

Marcy

Coarse salt, for coating

1   lime wedge

1½   cups peeled, pitted, and sliced fresh or partially thawed frozen peaches (page 148)

½   cup tequila

½   cup freshly squeezed lime juice

⅓   cup triple sec

3   tablespoons freshly squeezed lemon juice

2   tablespoons sugar

1   tablespoon grenadine syrup

3   cups ice

4   fresh mint leaves or lime or peach slices, for garnish (optional)

Make a small mound of salt on a saucer. To prepare the glasses, rub the lime wedge (or spent lime peels after juicing) along the rims of 4 margarita glasses. Before the rims dry, invert each glass in the salt and rotate it to coat the circumference of the rim with salt. Put the glasses in the freezer to chill.

Combine the peaches, tequila, lime juice, triple sec, lemon juice, sugar, grenadine syrup, and ice in a blender and process until smooth.

Pour into the prepared glasses, float a mint leaf on each serving, and serve immediately.

Cook's Note: You may use 1½ cups fresh or frozen Peach Puree (page 49) for the peaches.

CHAPTER THREE

At the Table
SAVORY DISHES and FAMILY FARMING

*"What do you do with lots of peaches?
You cook, you bake, you eat, you give life."*

—MARCY

Names of Old Friends / BY MAS

PEACH VARIETIES have evolved over the years. In California, massive shifts have mirrored significant national trends. For example, in 1977, California farmers led the nation and grew over 11 million boxes (each box is about twenty-three pounds). One of the major varieties grown was the Elberta, including the very popular Fay Elberta. Almost 1.5 million boxes of this variety were harvested in California. One out of ten peaches was in the Elberta family.

Elbertas lacked bright red color, didn't always ship well, and could bruise easily, however. Times changed and just two years later, in 1979, Elberta production dropped in half. Today, Elbertas account for less than 0.5 percent of the California peach crop—a small drop in the sea of twenty-four million boxes grown annually in California. Nowadays, only six of the forty major peach varieties grown in 1977 are still around and have a large enough market share to be counted in statewide statistics. Like most of the peach varieties on our farm, the remaining members of that original forty fall into the "other" category.

What happened to the dozens and dozens of good old peach varieties harvested in past decades? A few are grown by select farmers. Most are gone. The one tree in a farmer's backyard, usually a favorite variety, has been swept away, along with old farmhouses and dysfunctional barns. We have more and more farms without families and their farmhouses today.

My father called old fruit varieties "old friends." He carefully trained the trees, worked tenaciously to grow them, and together, my father and his orchards of peaches and nectarines, established our family farm. Now, I inherit his old friends.

Sun Crest, J. H. Hale, Red Haven

These are old peach varieties that almost no one grows anymore. They lacked full color and were cursed with short shelf life. In other words, they won't stay firm in cold storage for years—or whatever the current industry standard is. Newer varieties are bred for lipstick-red color and the ability to stay rock hard for weeks. Old fruits are obsolete, along with their farmers.

I cling to these heirloom varieties like friends. Most are gone from other orchards, but we try to rescue them on our farm—to find homes for homeless peaches. Our fields feel like memorials to the past. I too feel old and forgotten.

Regina, Flavor Crest, Royal Haven

While cleaning up one evening, I discovered an old Maxwell House coffee can sitting high on a shelf in the barn, tucked out of the way. Inside the powder blue tin, my father had saved the hand stamps from our fruit-packing days. I read the names out loud; the sounds of old fruit varieties echoed once again in the still air of the evening. I felt like I was reciting a list of our neighboring farmers who are no longer with us: Kamm Oliver, Al Riffel, Kei Hiyama.

When I was a child, I worked with these stamps every summer. My job was to press the names onto wooden boxes. The stamp handles were worn smooth from use over the years. The rubber lettering still held sawdust from the past. As a child, I often had to clean out the fine wood particles with a nail at the start of the work day. I remember my fingers were stained with purple ink all season long. One summer I proudly wore the stamp Forty-Niner, a cling-peach variety, boldly embossed on my arm like a farm boy's tattoo.

Elberta, Rio Oso Gem, Loring

We once knew peaches by their names. You would hear a shopper at the store call out, "Are the Elbertas ready?" The names sound like a greeting extended to an old friend. Elbertas once brought families together during the summer, for a canning and jamming tradition that bound the generations each year.

But today, with hundreds of new varieties introduced, fruits have lost their names and identities. A peach is a peach is a peach. The market says so.

Baby Crawford, Angelus, Babcock

Some old varieties had flaws. They were small, oddly shaped, prone to split pits. Others did not tolerate weather swings. A rainy spring resulted in brown rot. A summer heat wave caused fruits to ripen unevenly with easily bruised tips. Many varieties were discarded for these reasons, dismissed by a modern marketplace that rewards size, looks, and shelf life. We live in a world that wants young and firm peaches.

The old hand stamps help me connect with a different time and place and the meaning of our family farm. My father taught me to farm with a passion for taste, with the hope that our fruits create that moment of recognition during a hot summer day, a pause to enjoy flavor in our lives.

We farm memories—fruits that catapult you into recognitions of things past. If we're successful, it's not about our fruits but instead about a personalized story of taste. People remember great peaches. I hope they never forget their names or the names of their farmers.

A great peach can transport you to someplace else: the memory of a tree in a grandfather's backyard; a recollection of a mother and daughter in a summer kitchen canning peach halves or making jam; a visit to a farm where you lost your peach virginity and tasted flavor for the first time. These stories join our meals—wonderful foods that provide a social connection to places and people.

Gold Dust, Muir, Nectar

The names sound like poetry. They roll off my tongue as I imagine the juices and tastes filling my senses. Saying them makes me feel young.

I will find a way to use those old stamps on our farm. With a new generation on the land, we will add new ones to honor the past, putting them in the coffee can that holds the names of old friends.

COLD PEACH SOUP

MAKES 2 CUPS; SERVES 4

As noted earlier, we had a fortieth birthday party for our Sun Crest peaches at which several amazing chefs from the Bay Area prepared their favorite peach dishes. That was the first time I had ever seen or tasted a cold peach soup, which was made by Jesse Cool. Inspired by her dish, I thought it would be fun to create my own version. This soup, which makes a delightful starter to a meal, needs to be chilled for at least an hour before serving. If you are entertaining a crowd, serve in chilled shot glasses.

Marcy

1   medium carrot (about 1/2 cup), peeled and sliced

1   cup Peach Puree (recipe follows)

1/2   teaspoon peeled and grated fresh ginger

1   to 2 teaspoons freshly squeezed lime juice

1/2   cup plain Greek yogurt

2   tablespoons half-and-half
    Salt

1/4   cup sliced almonds, for garnish (optional)

Place the carrots in a small saucepan, add water to cover, and cook over medium heat for 5 to 7 minutes, until the carrots are easily pierced with the tip of a knife. Remove the pan from the heat and let the carrots cool in the liquid.

Place the cooled carrots and 1/2 cup cooking liquid in a blender and puree until smooth. Add the peach puree and pulse until fully mixed. Add the ginger, 1 teaspoon lime juice, yogurt, and half-and-half and puree until well blended. Transfer the soup to a bowl, cover tightly, and refrigerate for at least 1 hour to chill thoroughly.

Put the almonds in a dry skillet over medium heat and toast, tossing often, until golden, just a few minutes. Alternatively, spread the almonds on a baking sheet and toast in a preheated 350°F oven, stirring them once or twice, for 10 to 15 minutes, until golden. Pour onto a dish and let cool.

After the soup has chilled, season to taste with salt, and adjust with more lime juice if needed to balance the acidity of the peach puree. Ladle the soup into bowls and garnish with the almonds.

Peach Puree

MAKES ABOUT 1 CUP

Peach puree has many uses, especially in beverages, soups, and sauces, and is the perfect way to use up your extra-ripe peaches—the gushers. What's most important is that the peaches are flavorful, soft, and sweet! Unripe peaches will not puree well in a blender and will not give you the smooth product you are looking for.

Marcy

2   fresh gushy peaches, or 1 cup frozen or canned peaches (page 148 or 134, respectively)

To make the puree from fresh peaches, peel, pit, and quarter the peaches and drop into a blender. If using frozen peaches, thaw them, drain off the excess liquid, and then drop them into the blender. If using canned peaches, drain them well before measuring, reserving the syrup for another use, then drop them into the blender. Whirl the peaches until a smooth, silky puree forms.

Use the puree immediately, or seal it in a zip-top plastic bag, label the bag, and store in the freezer for up to a year.

PEACH GAZPACHO

Inspiration occasionally manifests itself in a mad scientist sort of fashion. This recipe is proof of that. I locked myself in the kitchen with a basket of vegetables from the refrigerator and a bucket of peaches until I came up with an exciting peach dish. With wild determination and some heat, a peach version of Spain's popular summer soup was born. I remember when my mom came home that day and I rushed out to greet her with a huge spoonful of my recent creation: a willing tester, my mom's eyes lit up with her first gulp. The experiment worked! Enjoy this savory soup ice cold as a starter or as a refresher between courses.

Nikiko

6	soft to gushy peaches (about 2 1/2 pounds), peeled, pitted, and quartered
1/2	cucumber, peeled, seeded, and cut into chunks
1	small clove garlic, minced
1	tablespoon champagne or golden balsamic vinegar
2	tablespoon extra-virgin olive oil, plus more for drizzling
1/2	teaspoon coarse salt
1/4	teaspoon freshly ground pepper
1/2	to 3/4 cup water
2	tablespoons coarsely chopped fresh cilantro or flat-leaf parsley
	Red bell pepper slices and avocado slices, for garnish (optional)

In a food processor, combine the peaches, cucumber, garlic, vinegar, oil, salt, pepper, and 1/2 cup water and pulse until coarsely pureed. Thin with the remaining 1/4 cup water if needed for a good consistency. Transfer to a bowl, cover, and refrigerate for at least 2 hours to chill thoroughly.

Just before serving, taste and adjust the seasoning with more vinegar, salt, and pepper if needed. Stir in the cilantro. Ladle into bowls, drizzle each serving with a little oil, and garnish with the bell pepper and avocado. Serve at once.

PEACH BRUSCHETTA

This recipe is ideal for mid- to late season in our family. That's not because of the peach varieties or the availability of the other ingredients, but because by then all of us have gotten to the point at which our bodies are telling us to slow down, to stop eating so many peaches! Living on a peach farm means we eat more peaches than maybe we should, but we can't help it. So when we're a couple of months into the harvest and we've got peach juice in our veins, this starter or light snack is the perfect way to savor the season mindfully with just a bite of fresh peach among a medley of lively flavors.

Nikiko

ARUGULA PESTO

1   clove garlic

1/4   cup walnuts

1/4   cup extra-virgin olive oil

1 1/2   cups arugula

     Salt and freshly ground pepper

1   tablespoon olive oil, plus more for brushing the bread

1   red onion, thinly sliced

1   teaspoon minced fresh rosemary

1   baguette, sliced 3/8 inch thick

1   to 2 cloves garlic, smashed

2   soft small peaches, peeled, halved, pitted, and cut into wedges 1/4 inch thick

     Shaved Parmesan cheese, for garnish

     Coarse salt

To make the pesto, combine the garlic and walnuts in a small food processor and pulse until finely chopped. Add the oil and arugula and continue to pulse until the mixture is evenly moist and spreadable. Season to taste with salt and pepper.

To make the bruschetta, heat the oil in large skillet over medium heat. Add the onion and rosemary. Cook for 20 minutes, stirring often, until the onion is soft. Set aside.

Meanwhile, prepare a medium-hot fire in a gas or charcoal grill. When the fire is ready, paint each bread slice on both sides with oil. Arrange the bread on the grill rack and toast, turning once, for about 2 minutes on each side, until golden brown. (If you do not have a grill, toast the bread on both sides in a preheated broiler until golden brown.)

When the bread slices are ready, let them cool enough to handle, then rub the smashed garlic cloves on both sides of each slice. Spread about 1 teaspoon of the pesto on one side of each bread slice. (You will need only 1/2 cup pesto; cover and store any remaining pesto in the refrigerator for another use.) Top each slice with some of the caramelized onion, 1 or 2 peach slices, a little Parmesan, and a sprinkle of salt. Serve warm or at room temperature.

CAPRESE with PEACHES

I invented this dish one summer evening after reflecting on how disappointed I was with the tomatoes I had in a traditional *caprese* at an Italian restaurant. My disappointment sparked an idea: if you can't find good tomatoes but have great peaches, why not substitute? So, I made the dish with peaches the first time for one of our Sunday family dinners. Everyone loved it! What I like best about it is that it's simple, delightful, and anyone who can use a knife can make it.

Marcy

1 (8-ounce) ball fresh mozzarella cheese
1 medium-large or 2 small peaches with give
8 fresh basil leaves
Extra-virgin olive oil, for drizzling
Kosher salt and freshly ground pepper

Cut the mozzarella into 8 slices, each about $1/4$ inch thick. Peel, halve, and pit the peach(es), then cut into slices about $1/4$ inch thick, yielding 16 slices total. On a serving plate, arrange the cheese, basil leaves, and peaches in a fan pattern, alternating them in that order. If you have used small peaches, use 2 slices for each basil leaf–cheese combination. Lightly drizzle with olive oil, sprinkle with salt and pepper, and serve.

VARIATIONS: For a heartier salad, add slices of vine-ripened tomatoes and arrange all of the elements on a bed of lettuce leaves. Drizzle with balsamic vinegar in addition to the oil. For a sandwich, layer the mozzarella, peach slices, and basil leaves along with prosciutto on sliced ciabatta or other Italian bread.

BUTTER LETTUCE CUPS with PEACHES and BLUE CHEESE

While attending graduate school at the University of Texas at Austin, I experienced what real humidity feels like for the first time. (We're lucky on the farm, as the Central Valley heat is incredibly dry.) To cope, I searched for foods and restaurants that helped me forget how sticky and uncomfortable I felt. When we could afford it, my student friends and I found ourselves at a small French restaurant, Justine's, tucked away on the east side of town. Laughter and a long meal was the cure to our humid and stressful days as students. This is my take on one of the restaurant's most refreshing salads. Making it in California is not the same, of course, as the climate and company have changed. But I still love the crunch and simplicity of this salad and the smiling faces I remember. If you are not a fan of blue cheese, replace it with a milder fresh cheese like ricotta and add more salt and pepper.

Nikiko

DRESSING

Juice of 1 lemon

3 tablespoons extra-virgin olive oil

Salt and freshly ground pepper

1 small head butter or Bibb lettuce

1 peach with give, halved, pitted, and sliced

1/2 cup walnuts, toasted and chopped

1 1/2 to 2 ounces blue cheese, crumbled

To make the dressing, stir together the lemon juice and oil, then stir in salt and pepper to taste.

Separate the lettuce leaves, selecting 4 to 6 leaves that form a nice cup shape, then rinse and pat dry. If the leaves are not very crisp, plunge them into ice water for a few minutes, drain, and pat dry.

Place the lettuce leaves in a large bowl, drizzle with the dressing, and toss gently to coat evenly.

Place each lettuce cup in the center of a salad plate. Fan an equal number of the peach slices on one side of each cup. Dividing them evenly, sprinkle the walnuts and blue cheese inside the cups. Serve immediately.

PROSCIUTTO-WRAPPED PEACHES

SERVES 4

As I worked on this recipe, I pondered the question, who is the author of a dish? I have eaten similar and even identical versions of this appetizer at many shared meals. The first time was at the house of my friend Kristine Kidd, who had adopted one of our Elberta peach trees. She generously shared the peaches she picked from our farm with us, the farm family. It was a moment of circular giving and shared joy, and the boundaries of whose dish it was were unclear in a wonderful way. Perhaps there are new ways to think about cooking, eating, and attribution. I appreciate it when a chef lists the names of the farms that provided the raw materials for the dishes on the menu. Although this naming ritual is always incomplete— for example, I have never seen farmworkers' names or the names of the truck drivers who deliver the food—it still provokes something good in me. As a farmer, I feel honored when our family name is cited, and as an eater, I am reminded that many more people are involved in my food than are physically present at my table. Recognition creates more gratitude. Like so many creative tasks, I believe cooking is a process of drawing on shared knowledge and ideas, of borrowing and building on others' work. We tap into a lineage of food knowledge and experiences to create so-called new dishes. This recipe is just my iteration. I invite you to create your own. In the material world, it seems that comprehensive attribution is necessarily difficult and arbitrary (How many people touch a peach from farm to mouth? Who counts as an author of a meal?), but I still think recognition is important, especially because I believe gratitude can be infinite.

Nikiko

1   medium-large peach with give, peeled, halved, pitted, and cut into 8 wedges

8   large fresh basil leaves

4   slices prosciutto, each cut lengthwise into two 1-inch-wide strips

Wrap each peach wedge with a basil leaf and then with a strip of prosciutto. Arrange on a platter or divide among individual plates and serve.

Peach Fever / BY MAS

WE CATCH IT, it invades our logic, overriding rational thought, disrupting our best-laid plans. It spreads and settles in our psyche, our emotions swell, the heart races. We call it peach fever, a love of our work and the land that burdens us with a sense of responsibility and caring. Peach fever curses us, especially when weather disasters challenge our spirit and bad prices inject a cold reality into our love affair. Peach fever can destroy and transform and lives on our farm throughout the year.

Frost

The cold front moves in from the Artic, and local forecasts predict temperatures in the high twenties. But this is early spring on the farm, when March peach blossoms are in their glory. The cold settles on the delicate pink flowers and I smell death. We respond with water, warm water at about 50°F that we pump from the earth. We spread it like a warm blanket over the earth. With luck, the flowers will live. By sunrise, I'm beat but happy to see fog blanketing the earth as warm pump water mixes with cold air and produces mist. A good sign, fog means the air is above freezing. I can now rest.

Spring Rains

Peaches are native to the high deserts of China. They don't like rain, especially in the warm spring air, which, when combined with heavy moisture, becomes a breeding ground for diseases like brown rot.

Pathogens trick you because you can't see them. Brown rot fungus grows with the moisture and warmth, but the peach itself looks normal. Ironically, when the fruit begins to sweeten, the rot thrives on the added sugars and explodes like a cancer in the fruit.

We try various organic treatments to counteract the disease. Better yet, we work with peach varieties that don't seem to be as susceptible to rot. Older varieties, especially those with lots of fuzz, appear more resistant. I like to think that the thick fuzz acts as a natural defense mechanism, protecting the flesh because water doesn't stick to the surface as readily—nature's way of self-defense.

The Heat Wave

We can have summer temperatures up to 115°F on our farm. Ripening fruit often goes soft, especially at the tips and stem-end shoulders. Harvest becomes a race, trying to pick as much as possible as the fruits seem to ripen all at once. But we are human and we can neither expect workers nor ourselves to put in long days in such heat. We'll start at five o'clock in the morning but have to stop by noon. Bodies are spent, we can't drink enough fluids to compensate, legs cramp at night from exertion.

But we go out the next day and the day after. There is no choice. Peaches need to be picked. It's what must be done. And sometimes, the peach trees understand too. In extreme heat, they may also shut down, delay ripening, and the fruits can stay firm on the tree. It's as if they take pity on the farmer. Imagine, empathy from a peach tree. What better friend can a farmer have?

Bad Prices and Bad People

Bad prices challenge you the most. We've had disasters when too many peaches flood the market and the prices plummet. You know better but can't help it and take it personally: lousy prices must mean that no one wants your fruits—in other words, no one wants you. It hurts.

I once wrote about this plight for the *Los Angeles Times*, sharing my frustrations and anger about peaches that were worth five cents a pound. I wanted to quit farming. I then got a note from a reader asking me in what store could she get some of my five-cents-a-pound peaches. Insulting.

Hail in June

Once, just before our best peaches were to be harvested, an extremely rare hailstorm struck our valley. I stood out in the yard screaming at the dark, dark clouds, which answered with a flash of lightening and pounding thunder. The winds blew the sheets of rain sideways, then the ice balls crashed down from the heavens. The icy stones fell from the sky, slicing and dicing the helpless peaches. In ten minutes, we lost tens of thousands of dollars.

I drove the quarter mile to my folks' place. My father was sweeping hail out of his shed. We stood silently as we watched the storm strike another farmer to the east and then another. "It's never hailed like this in June," he said. "Never." We shared our first disaster together that day.

Without family, we could not survive these challenges. When things go wrong, we all feel responsible and grieve together. Then we trudge out into the fields the next day and start over. We all have peach fever and will learn to live with it.

PANKO-FRIED PEACHES

SERVES 4 TO 6

I call this hapa food. The term *hapa* is deliciously slippery. It is often used to describe mixed-race Japanese Americans but not always. For me, being hapa provides a way of claiming a whole racial and ethnic identity as opposed to thinking of myself as "just" or "only" half-and-half. I am a whole person, and my experience of race, culture, and nationality is more complicated than adding fractions. This dish did not emerge from a place of separation in which two disparate things were fused together, but rather from the co-constitution, interdependence, and wholeness of my life as a hapa growing peaches in the United States and cooking food from my multiple cultural and racial lineages that go far beyond this country's borders. I have learned to make and cook my own path. Biting into this treat is like unleashing a burst of glowing peach wrapped in a crunchy cocoon. This could be served as a side dish with other tempura, on top of a salad, or even with green tea ice cream and chile-infused honey as a dessert. When we step outside of rigid categories, possibilities are infinite, no?

Nikiko

Canola oil, for deep-frying

5 to 6 soft large peaches, peeled and halved

All-purpose flour, for dredging

2 eggs, beaten

2 cups panko

Pour the oil to a depth of at least 3 inches into a deep-fryer, wok, or deep, heavy saucepan and heat to 300°F.

Meanwhile, cut the peaches into 1/2-inch-thick slices. Spread the flour on a plate and spread the *panko* on a second plate.

When the oil is ready, using chopsticks or tongs, dredge a peach slice in the flour, shaking off the excess, and then dip in the egg, allowing the excess to drip off. Finally, dredge the slice in the *panko*, covering it as evenly as possible with the light flakes.

Carefully place the peach slice in the hot oil. It should immediately begin to bubble and hiss. While the first slice is cooking, continue to dredge and dip more slices in the flour, egg, and *panko* and add them to the oil. Fry no more than 3 or 4 slices at a time, making sure they do not touch one another, for about 1 minute, until evenly golden. Using a wire skimmer, transfer the finished slices to a wire rack set over a shallow bowl or pan to drain briefly. Serve piping hot.

PEACH DAY PICKLES

MAKES 1 CUP (ENOUGH FOR 4 TO 6 SANDWICHES)

In 2011, I took my first trip to Japan with my mom, dad, and brother. We visited relatives in the small village of Takamura in Kumamoto prefecture where one of my great-grandmothers was born and spent her childhood. Driving from the train station to the family farmhouse, I looked out the window to see a flat, sweeping basin of cultivated land under the protective gaze of distant mountains. I felt at home. The scene looked similar to the view from our farm in the Central Valley, bordered by the towering Sierra Nevada. Many years ago, as my *o-baasan* (great-grandmother) worked on the same land that I work today, I wonder if she looked up at the Sierra and thought for a second that she, too, was home. But she lived and toiled in these fields when anti-Asian racism was legalized in the early twentieth century by the California Alien Land Laws of 1913 and 1920 that prohibited Asian immigrants from owning land in the state. Asians were not wanted, not welcomed. And yet, here I am, a fourth-generation Japanese American and I call this place home.

The roots of this recipe come from *tsunomono*, a lightly pickled Japanese cucumber salad I grew up eating. I wish I could share it with my *o-baasan*; I wonder if her spirit is still in these fields imagining that she is home. Serve these pickles as a condiment, a salad, on a salad, or on a sandwich. We have enjoyed them tucked between slices of ciabatta with roast beef, roasted poblano chile, arugula, and a mild cheese like Fontina, fresh goat, or provolone.

Nikiko

1 peach, firm or with give, peeled, halved, pitted, and sliced 1/4 inch thick

1 tablespoon cider vinegar

1/2 teaspoon whole-grain mustard

Put the peach slices in a small bowl. In a second small bowl, stir together the vinegar and mustard, mixing well. Pour the mixture over the peaches and toss gently to coat. Cover and refrigerate for 2 hours before serving.

SUMMER FRESH FRUIT SALAD

SERVES 4 TO 6

Not all dishes have to be complicated to be sexy or appealing. My approach to cooking falls on the simple and unadulterated side of the spectrum, relying on the natural beauty and honest flavor (or personality) of the primary ingredients. When it comes to pairing foods with fresh peaches, fewer competing elements are best for me. I like sliced fresh peaches with oatmeal, granola, or other dry cereal, and/or yogurt for breakfast; on meringues, angel food cake, or ice cream for dessert; and with a combination of other summer fruits for a side dish.

In fact, summer really isn't summer without fruit salad. I like to use fruits that are at their peak of season, balancing sweet with tart, soft with crunchy, and mixing a variety of colors. In this recipe, I use Thompson seedless grapes (which we grow on the farm) or honeydew melon for the green ingredient. Whether you decide to use grapes or melon chunks, make sure they are sweet and green or yellow-green. Our grapes are small, so I don't cut them. If I were buying large green grapes, I might slice them in half. The berries add red and blue and a tartness to contrast with the sweet. Because bananas, apples, nectarines, and peaches oxidize when cut, I work with them last and squeeze the lime juice over them as soon as they are in the bowl.

Marcy

DRESSING

½ cup plain or flavored yogurt

1 tablespoon honey

1 cup Thompson seedless grapes or honeydew melon chunks

1 cup halved or quartered strawberries or whole raspberries

1 cup blueberries, boysenberries, or blackberries

1 cup pineapple, banana, or apple chunks

1 large nectarine or 2 plums, pitted and sliced

1 large peach with give, peeled, halved, pitted, and sliced

Grated zest and juice of 1 lime

Sugar, for sweetening (optional)

To make the dressing, in a small bowl, stir together the yogurt and honey to blend fully.

To make the salad, gently layer the fruits in a large, clear-glass bowl in the following order: grapes, berries, pineapple, nectarine, and finally peaches. Sprinkle the lime zest over the fruit, and then squeeze the lime juice over the top. With a large spoon, gently mix the ingredients to coat evenly with the lime juice. Sprinkle on the sugar, depending on the sweetness of your ingredients, and mix again gently.

Just before serving, drizzle the dressing over the salad, or serve the dressing in a bowl alongside the salad.

Pheromones / BY MAS

THE FARMWORKERS CALL IT "medicine" for our trees. We call it pheromone control, the use of a highly sophisticated science to stop insect damage on peaches. It's a time for family work and family conversations in the fields. My kids joke about their father's attempt at sex education.

Three worm pests attack our peaches: oriental fruit moth, omnivorous leafroller, and peach twig borer. Conventional farmers spray harsh chemicals to rid their peaches of these pests. Organic farmers use a much softer approach, one involving pheromones, a scent that triggers a social response. In our case, each female moth of these three worm pests secretes a specific scent that attracts the male for the purposes of mating.

Each year, the family gathers to treat the farm against worm pests. We spend a few days in the orchard, placing pheromone strips in each peach tree. These small, thin plastic strips are about $1^1/_2$ inches wide and 3 inches long and have a small plastic hook stapled to the top. Each strip has a small black dot about $^3/_4$ inch in diameter, made from a thin membrane with tiny, tiny holes that allows it to breathe. A small amount, less than an ounce, of pheromone is inside each strip, and over the course of weeks, the scent is gradually emitted.

I remember years ago first explaining this farm job to the children when I thought they were old enough to understand, offering them a lesson on organic farming and how these strips work. As we hung each strip high in a tree, I told them to imagine that the entire orchard is filled with this perfume of the female. The male smells this scent and is confused because he can't find the female. Without mating, there are no eggs and no worms. Thus, we have pest control.

Nikiko and Korio claimed I skipped a few steps. I repeated my explanation and realized this is a lesson on birth control in the orchards.

Each strip contains the specific scent of the female. The oriental fruit moth has a different smell than the peach twig borer. That's why we hang three different strips to target the three worm peach pests.

The children rolled their eyes, waiting for the good stuff.

In other words, the males get a whiff of this perfume and get excited. They buzz our orchard, believing some hot females are waiting for them.

The children nodded but wanted me to be more explicit.

Okay, the male moths think they'll get lucky. They fly into our peach orchard singles bar looking for sex. They believe some females must be in heat and in the mood.

Now I had the kids' attention.

The males are horny as hell, but with this scent everywhere, they can't find the females to pick up, and in the end they leave alone.

Korio thought they must be overwhelmed and give up. I agreed.

Nikiko and Marcy laughed and added that the males are simply lost and disoriented and that's nothing new: confused males. (Actually, the peach industry calls this the confusion method of worm control.)

Nothing is killed except a lot of anticipation along with some broken hearts.

Nikiko chimed in that this creates a lot of frustrated males. Marcy laughed.

I concurred, trying to describe what this means for our peaches. With no mating, there are no eggs and thus no worms to eat our fruits.

Korio and Nikiko called it the ultimate "safe sex." For a protective father of then teenagers, that observation made me smile.

The kids asked if there are human pheromones. I joked that if I knew that for sure, I'd make a zillion dollars.

Nikiko pondered and then announced that pheromones act as a type of repellant. They repel because the males seek too hard.

I liked her contrarian view. Still thinking of the human pheromone, I started coining advertising slogans: They distract because they attract. The more he tries, the more he dies.

I concluded that I could market the human pheromone as a high-tech rhythm method and make my target consumers fathers at the moment that they discover that their little girls have grown up to be pretty young teenagers. I smell a fortune.

PEACH and NECTARINE SALSA

I know summer has arrived when I try to find things to eat with fresh fruit salsa for breakfast, lunch, and dinner. This salsa screams "It's summer!" loud and clear. Our family enjoys it in egg burritos or atop grilled or broiled chicken breasts, salmon fillets, salmon burgers, or fish.

Marcy

1	large or 2 medium peaches with give, peeled, halved, pitted, and diced
2	nectarines, pitted and diced
1/2	cup fresh cilantro leaves, chopped
1/2	red bell pepper, seeded and diced
1/2	red onion, diced (yellow or green onions may be substituted)
1	small-medium jalapeño chile, seeded and finely diced
	Juice of 1 lime (1 to 2 tablespoons)
	Chili powder, for seasoning
	Salt and freshly ground pepper

In a bowl, combine the peach(es), nectarines, cilantro, bell pepper, onion, and chile. Drizzle with the lime juice and season lightly with the chili powder, salt, and pepper. Serve immediately with your favorite dish.

VARIATION: To turn this salsa into a salad, add diced avocado, cucumber, jicama, mango, and/or papaya and serve on a bed of lettuce.

Cook's Note: Be careful when working with jalapeño chiles, as they contain compounds that can burn your skin. You may want to wear rubber gloves (or slip plastic bags over your hands) when working with the cut chiles to avoid burning your fingers. Also make sure you do not touch your eyes, nose, or other sensitive areas when handling chiles. (I once accidentally put in my contact lenses with jalapeño-laced fingers and my eyes burned for hours!)

SPINACH SALAD with PEACHES and PEACH VINAIGRETTE

Our tree adoption guests enjoyed this simple salad as part of a brunch we served on harvest day under the peach trees in 2011. With the help of friends as volunteers, we made enough salad for our 250 guests and found that we had about twice the amount of spinach and vinaigrette we needed! I have since adjusted the proportions, so you should not have too much left over. You'll notice the quantity for the red onion is a range. How much you use depends on the size of the onion. If you have a very large red onion, you will only need one-fourth of it; if the onion is small, use one-half of it. As with any salad, if you have another favorite ingredient in the refrigerator that you would like to add, do it!

Marcy

VINAIGRETTE

2 tablespoons Peach Jam (page 137)

2 tablespoons freshly squeezed orange juice

1 tablespoon freshly squeezed lemon or lime juice or golden balsamic vinegar

2 tablespoons canola oil

1 tablespoon water

1/8 teaspoon salt

4 cups organic spinach leaves

1/4 to 1/2 red onion, thinly sliced and separated into slivers

2 firm small peaches or nectarines, peeled if using peaches, halved, pitted, and thinly sliced

1/4 cup roasted sunflower seeds
Freshly ground pepper

To make the vinaigrette, combine all of the ingredients in a small jar, cap tightly, and shake vigorously until well mixed. Alternately, you can use your blender to combine the ingredients.

In a large salad bowl, combine the spinach, onion, and peaches. Drizzle with the vinaigrette and toss to coat evenly. Divide the salad among salad plates, sprinkle with the sunflower seeds and a few grinds of pepper, and serve immediately.

VARIATION: Add some crumbled feta cheese or fresh goat cheese to make this more of a main dish salad.

SUMMER THAI SHRIMP and NOODLE SALAD

One of the best things about living in California's Central Valley is the rich ethnic diversity of the region. Immigrants from all over the world have been arriving in the area for generations. In the years following the Vietnam War, many Southeast Asians settled in and around the city of Fresno and are now our neighbors and friends. They have contributed to the community in many ways and have taken up many professions. Some of them have started farms, and others have established restaurants that we enjoy. This recipe was inspired by a lunch at one of my favorite Thai restaurants. It combines the freshness and spiciness of Thai food with our valley peaches, creating a fusion that says, "This is California cuisine."

This recipe uses the dried thin rice noodles mostly commonly labeled *maifun*, their Cantonese name. Many different brands of *maifun* are found in Asian groceries and in the Asian food section of supermarkets. The best ones to use are quite thin and look like string or thick thread. I like *maifun* packaged by Yatta!, a Japanese company, the best. If you cannot find *maifun*, you can use thin rice noodles that are about 1/8 inch thick or *saifun*, dried thin noodles made from mung bean starch. Follow the instructions on the package for cooking the noodles (or softening in hot water), as brands vary.

Marcy

DRESSING

- 2 tablespoons light brown sugar
- 3 tablespoons freshly squeezed lime juice
- 2 tablespoons fish sauce
- 1 tablespoon canola oil
- 1½ teaspoons chili paste, or ½ teaspoon red pepper flakes
- 1 teaspoon toasted sesame oil
- 1½ teaspoons peeled and grated fresh ginger
- 2 cloves garlic, minced

To make the dressing, in a small bowl, stir together all the ingredients, mixing well. (Alternatively, combine all the ingredients in a jar, cap tightly, and shake vigorously to mix well.) Set aside to allow the flavors to meld.

To make the salad, cook the noodles according to the package directions. They are ready when they are like al dente pasta, not dry in the middle and not mushy. (Yatta! brand calls for cooking the noodles in 4 cups of boiling water over medium heat for 4 minutes.) Drain the noodles in a colander, rinse with cold water, and drain again, shaking the colander to remove any excess water.

4   ounces maifun (dried thin rice
    noodles)

2   cups bean sprouts or blanched
    snow peas

1/2 bell pepper (yellow, orange, red, or
    green), seeded and thinly sliced

3   green onions, white and green parts,
    thinly sliced on the diagonal

1   cup fresh cilantro leaves, torn in half

1/2 cup fresh Asian basil or sweet basil
    leaves, torn in half

3   fresh peaches with give, peeled,
    halved, pitted, and sliced 1/4 inch
    thick or cut into 1/2-inch cubes, or
    2 cups diced canned or frozen
    peaches (pages 134 or 148,
    respectively) in the off-season

    Salt and freshly ground pepper

    Fish sauce and chile paste, for
    seasoning (optional)

    Chopped peanuts, for garnish
    (optional)

SHRIMP

1   tablespoon canola oil

12 to 18 large (size 41–50 or bigger)
    shrimp, peeled

1   clove garlic, minced

Transfer the drained noodles to a large salad bowl, add the bean sprouts, bell pepper, onions, cilantro, and basil, reserving a little of the cilantro and/or basil for garnish. Add the peaches and dressing and toss gently with tongs. Season with salt and pepper, then taste and adjust with the fish sauce and chili paste.

To prepare the shrimp, place a wok or deep skillet over medium-high heat and add the oil. When the oil is hot, add the shrimp and garlic and stir-fry for about 3 minutes, until done. The shrimp are ready when they turn a salmon-pink on the outside and the meat is white and no longer translucent gray.

Divide the salad among individual plates, distributing the peaches evenly. Arrange the shrimp on top of the salads and then drizzle the salads with any pan drippings. Garnish with the reserved cilantro and/or basil and the peanuts and serve.

PIZZA with GRILLED PEACHES

MAKES 2 PIZZAS; SERVES 4 TO 5

In our family, when we sit down to eat we often say *Itadakimasu*, a common Japanese phrase recited before a meal. It roughly translates to "I receive." Like many folk traditions, its significance is open to interpretation. When I say the phrase, I think of it as a moment to awaken a mindful practice of eating in which I acknowledge both the people around the table with whom I am sharing a meal and the stories of farmers, farmworkers, and many other laborers whose wisdom and sweat bring us our food. Perhaps I should also say it before I cook, because recipes like this one are far from an individual endeavor. This pizza grew from a friend's recommendation to explore baking with a no-knead technique we learned from a cookbook by Jeff Hertzberg and Zoë François combined with my favorite way to cook in the summer, on the grill.

Nikiko

DOUGH

2   teaspoons active dry yeast
2   teaspoons sugar
1   teaspoon salt
1   tablespoon finely chopped fresh rosemary
1½ cups lukewarm water
¼   cup extra-virgin olive oil
3½ cups all-purpose flour, plus more for rolling out the dough

To make the dough, in an extra-large bowl, stir together the yeast, sugar, salt, rosemary, water, and oil. Let stand for a few minutes, until the yeast has dissolved. Add the flour and stir with a wooden spoon until evenly mixed. Loosely cover the bowl (make sure it is *not* airtight), place the bowl in a warm spot (around 80°F), and let rise for 2 hours. Then refrigerate the covered bowl for at least 4 hours, until the dough is thoroughly chilled. (The dough can be kept in the refrigerator for up to 1 week before continuing.)

If using a baking stone, place it on the center rack of the oven. Preheat the oven to 450°F.

- 2 tablespoons extra-virgin olive oil, plus more for brushing the grill rack
- 2 firm peaches, halved, and pitted
- 1 large red onion, thinly sliced
- 1 (8-ounce) can tomato sauce
  Large handful of arugula, lightly dressed with olive oil
- 4 ounces fresh goat cheese
  Freshly ground pepper

Prepare a medium fire in a charcoal or gas grill. Brush the grill rack with a light coating of oil. Place the peaches, cut side down, on the grill rack and grill for 6 to 7 minutes, until thick grill marks appear. Flip the peach halves over and grill for another 3 to 4 minutes, until the skin is loose around the edges. Remove from the grill, and when cool enough to handle, slice 1/4 inch thick, remove the peel, and set aside.

Heat 2 tablespoons of the oil in a large skillet over medium heat. Add the onion, cover, and cook slowly, stirring often, for 20 minutes, until the onion is soft. Set aside.

With floured hands, divide the dough in half. It will be very sticky and loose. Transfer half of the dough to a generously floured work surface (leave the other half in the bowl) and knead a few times to form into a disk. If you like thin-crust pizza, roll out the dough into round about 1/8 inch thick. If you prefer a thicker crust, roll out about 1/4 inch thick and form a slight rim around the edge. Transfer the dough round to a piece of parchment paper or to a baking sheet lined with parchment.

To assemble the pizza, spread half of the tomato sauce evenly over the dough round, leaving a border around the edge about 1/2 inch wide. Sprinkle half of the onions over the sauce, followed by half of the arugula. Using a spoon, drop dollops of half of the goat cheese over the arugula, spacing them evenly. Top with half of the peach slices, again spaced evenly.

If using a baking stone, slide the parchment with the pizza onto a baker's peel or an inverted baking sheet and then slide the pizza with the parchment onto the stone. If using a baking sheet, place on the center rack of the oven. Bake for 15 to 20 minutes, until the pizza is golden on the bottom.

While the first pizza is baking, assemble the second pizza with the remaining ingredients. When the first pizza is ready, remove it from the oven and slide in the second pizza. Top each pizza with a few grinds of pepper, then cut into wedges and serve hot.

SHAKING BEEF with PEACHES

🍑 SERVES 4

This Asian-Californian fusion recipe was inspired by our friend Mai Pham. Mai owns and operates Lemon Grass Restaurant in Sacramento, California, which specializes in Vietnamese cuisine and draws on her childhood roots in Vietnam and Thailand. We partnered with Mai to host a dinner titled Peaches at Lemon Grass, where she first introduced us to shaking beef with peaches. This recipe is our version, a humble offering in homage to our friendship with Mai. For the bed of greens, you may use a spring mix or other baby lettuces, or if you would like a peppery bite, use arugula. Serve this dish with stir-fried vegetables and your favorite rice for a refreshing summer meal. In our household, Mas likes Japanese short-grain white rice, I like short-grain brown rice, and Nikiko and Korio like a combination of both!

Marcy

BEEF AND MARINADE

12 ounces boneless beef sirloin (or better grade) steak, cut across the grain into bite-size pieces

1 tablespoon oyster sauce

2 cloves garlic, minced

1 1/2 teaspoons sugar

1/2 teaspoon freshly ground pepper

SALAD

2 tablespoons freshly squeezed lime juice

2 tablespoons rice vinegar

1 tablespoon fish sauce

1 tablespoon light soy sauce

1 tablespoon sugar

1/2 jalapeño chile, seeded and diced, or 1/2 teaspoon red pepper flakes

3 cups (about 2 ounces) organic mixed greens, torn into bite-size pieces

[MORE]

To marinate the beef, in a bowl, combine the beef, oyster sauce, garlic, sugar, and pepper and toss to coat the meat evenly. Let the meat rest for 20 minutes.

To make the salad, first make the vinaigrette. In a small bowl, stir together the lime juice, vinegar, fish sauce, soy sauce, sugar, and chile until the sugar dissolves. Set aside to allow the flavors to blend while you work on preparing the remainder of the recipe. (The vinaigrette can be made up to a day in advance, if desired.) Ready the greens and arrange them in a bed on a platter.

To cook the beef, heat the oil in a large wok or skillet over high heat. If you are working on a gas burner, add the beef to the pan all at once and stir-fry or shake for 3 to 4 minutes, until nicely browned. If you are using an electric burner, cook the beef in two batches to maintain a high temperature in the pan and minimize the accumulation of juices. If excess juice forms, remove the beef and leave the pan on the burner for a short time to evaporate it. When the meat is ready, turn off the

{CONTINUED}

{CONTINUED FROM PAGE 75}

2   tablespoons canola oil

2   peaches with give, peeled, halved, pitted, and cut into 1/4-inch-thick slices

1/4   large red onion, thinly sliced and separated into slivers

1/2   cup fresh Asian basil or sweet basil leaves, torn in half

heat, add the peaches, onion slices, and basil and toss to mix with the meat.

Arrange the beef mixture on the greens and drizzle the dish with the vinaigrette. Serve immediately.

Cook's Note: You'll find the fish sauce and oyster sauce in the Asian section of your supermarket or at an Asian specialty market. If you can't find fresh Asian basil or more the common sweet basil, you may substitute fresh mint leaves.

MUSTARD-PEACH GLAZED CHICKEN

SERVES 4

I think every cook has at least one story of how he or she destroyed a well-intentioned dish. In the Masumoto family, we have a penchant for burning things. My all-time memorable mess up was grilling chicken. I marinated a whole chicken with Meyer lemons and herbs and put it on the grill to roast. Everything was going well, until I got distracted in a conversation. Suddenly, I saw smoke rising from the grill: the entire chicken was on fire. When we cut the gas and snuffed the flames, I saw that the whole bird was charred black. I burst into tears. My mom wisely hugged me and chuckled. Luckily, my relationship with chicken did not end there and the levity of laughter was well learned. I'm still learning to master chicken on the grill, so here is a winter dish that is cooked in the oven and calls for peach preserves. I enjoy it accompanied with roasted brussels sprouts and wild rice.

Nikiko

GLAZE

1   teaspoon canola oil

1   shallot, finely chopped

1¹/₂ tablespoons cider vinegar

1¹/₂ tablespoons low-sodium soy sauce

³/₄ cup Peach Jam (page 137)

1   tablespoon Dijon mustard

1   tablespoon spicy mustard (such as Inglehoffer's Sweet Hot Mustard)

4   bone-in, skin-on chicken thighs
    Salt and freshly ground pepper
    All-purpose flour, for dredging

1   tablespoon canola oil

Preheat the oven to 350°F.

To make the glaze, heat the oil in a saucepan over medium heat. Add the shallot and cook, stirring, for 4 minutes, until softened. Mix in the vinegar, soy sauce, jam, and both mustards. Turn down the heat to low and cook, stirring occasionally, for 15 minutes. Remove from the heat, pass the glaze through a fine-mesh sieve, and discard the solids.

Sprinkle the chicken with salt and pepper, then dredge in the flour, shaking off the excess. Select an ovenproof skillet large enough to hold the thighs in a single layer. Heat the oil over medium-high heat. When the oil is hot, add the chicken and cook, turning once, for 3 to 4 minutes on each side, until browned.

Pour the glaze evenly over the chicken and cover the pan with aluminum foil. Place in the oven and bake for 20 minutes. Baste with the glaze in the pan, re-cover, and continue to bake for about 20 minutes longer, until cooked through. Let cool slightly before serving.

SPICE-RUBBED PORK CHOPS and GRILLED PEACHES

Pork and peaches are meant for each other. This recipe uses a simple spice rub to add flavor to the pork. You can personalize the spices and develop your own mix; try adding ground ginger or sweet paprika. Serve this dish with grilled vegetables, or slice the peaches and pork and serve them over lettuce to make a main-course salad. I like the pork chops best with grilled peaches, but you can use warm Peach Jam (page 137) in the off season.

Nikiko

4   boneless pork loin chops

2   teaspoons ground fennel or anise, or 2 teaspoons whole fennel seeds or aniseeds

2   teaspoons ground cumin or whole cumin seeds

2   tablespoons dried oregano

1/2 teaspoon freshly ground pepper

1/4 teaspoon salt

    Olive or canola oil, for brushing the grill rack

2   firm peaches, halved, and pitted

Remove the pork chops from the refrigerator and allow to come to room temperature. Prepare two zones: a medium and medium-hot fire in a charcoal or gas grill.

If using whole fennel and cumin seeds, toast in a dry pan over medium-low heat until fragrant. Let cool, then grind in a spice grinder or with a mortar and pestle.

To make the spice rub for the chops, mix together the fennel, cumin, oregano, pepper, and salt. Rub the spice mixture evenly on both sides of each chop.

When the grill is ready, brush the grill rack with a light coating of oil. To grill the peaches, place them, cut side down, on the grill rack and grill for 6 to 7 minutes, until nice grill marks appear. Flip the peach halves over and grill for another 3 to 4 minutes, until the skin is loose around the edges and grill marks appear on bottom. To grill the pork chops, place them on the medium-hot zone of the grill rack and grill on the first side for 6 to 7 minutes (or a few minutes longer if the cut is thicker than 3/4 inch). To add grill marks, rotate the chops 45 degrees after the first 2 to 3 minutes. Flip the chops and cook for 4 to 5 minutes on the second side, again rotating the chops 45 degrees after the first 2 minutes for grill marks, until cooked but still juicy. Serve immediately with the peaches.

Value of Work / BY MAS

I DEALLY, everyone shares our passion for farming peaches. But times have changed and squeezed farmers and their workers. According to the Bureau of Labor Statistics, in 1960, Americans spent 24 percent of their annual income on food. By 1984, it had dropped to 15 percent and in 2012 it was only 9 percent. Meanwhile, farmworker minimum wages in California have grown, from $1.00 per hour in 1960 to $3.35 per hour in 1984 and $8.00 per hour currently. For the farmer, margins are tighter and tighter, with people devoting less of their income to food while wages in the fields have grown.

Given the fact that there is less money for the farmer and higher costs, what's the proper wage for workers? Perhaps the model of how labor and social justice fit into the current farming economy has yet to be invented. Or, perhaps we will always struggle.

We used to pick peaches, pack them in boxes, and wave good-bye to them at the loading dock. We never followed them to market and we trusted the currency of money to determine their worth. Often, the only reaction we heard was a negative one, usually a buyer complaining about a problem with the peaches and asking for an adjustment in pricing.

Now I realize that sort of appraisal is wrong and devalues our work. We need to trust ourselves and believe price is only one part of the equation. We believe in a new emergence of value based on human and social capital. Perhaps we all need to calculate a well-being scale into our economies of life: joy, happiness, and passion have value and significance.

It takes a village to grow a peach. I can't do it myself, despite an economic system based on individual capitalist entrepreneurship. A great peach has to have partners, those who supply farm inputs like fertilizers and pest controls and those who help with the harvest, packing, shipping, and selling of a peach. We're all part of the journey of a peach from the farm to your table. We all should be in group therapy, too, as the system is complicated, highly human, and unpredictable. When it works, a perfect peach manifests a group hug from all of us along the food chain.

SLOW-COOKED PORK TACOS

🍑 SERVES 4 TO 6

As a farmer, seasonal cooking implies not only the type of things I cook but also the constraints on how I cook. During the summer, the heat dictates when we can work. We tend to work in two shifts, one in the early morning until we can no longer bear the sun, and then a second shift when the temperature breaks in the evening. We try to wring every drop of sunlight out of the day, which doesn't leave much time for cooking dinner. A slow cooker has been the perfect answer to my dual loves of farming and cooking. This dish is also perfect for parties or large dinners that require setup and preparation of other dishes. We like eating these tacos with a fresh salsa (like the Peach and Nectarine Salsa, page 67) and Peach Margaritas (page 41).

Nikiko

1 tablespoon canola oil

1 (2¹/₂-pound) boneless pork shoulder roast

1 tablespoon ground cumin

1 yellow onion, sliced

3 cloves garlic, minced

¹/₄ cup water

1 to 2 chipotle chiles in adobo sauce, or 1 tablespoon red pepper flakes

1 tablespoon dried oregano

1 teaspoon salt

1 (12-ounce) bottle beer (I like to use Pacifico or Negra Modelo)

4 firm to soft peaches, peeled, halved, and pitted

8 to 12 small corn tortillas, warmed, for serving

1¹/₂ to 2 cups thinly sliced cabbage

2 limes, cut into wedges

Peach and Nectarine Salsa (page 67), for serving (optional)

Heat the oil in a large skillet over medium-high heat. When the oil is hot, add the pork and cook for 2 to 3 minutes on each side, until browned. Transfer the pork to a slow cooker.

Add the cumin, onion, and garlic to the same skillet off the heat and warm, stirring occasionally, for 2 to 3 minutes, until fragrant. Pour the water into the skillet to loosen any spices or browned bits stuck to the pan bottom. Pour the contents of the skillet over the meat.

Add the chile(s), oregano, salt, beer, and peaches to the slow cooker, cover, and cook on high for 4 hours or on low for 6 to 8 hours. The meat is done when it easily falls apart with the gentle tug of a fork. Carefully shred the meat with two forks. Discard the juices, onions, and peaches or cool and store in the refrigerator for pork soup stock or other use.

To assemble each taco, layer 2 tortillas on top of each other and place about ¹/₄ cup of the meat in a mound on the tortillas, extending it across the middle. Add a little cabbage, a scoop of salsa, and a squeeze of lime juice. Serve warm.

ROLLED PORK LOIN

SERVES 6 TO 8

This is a favorite year-round Masumoto family main course for special occasions, from graduation parties to winter holidays. We still think of it as a seasonal dish because we use two kinds of preserved peaches that we make every summer. I also like this recipe because when I am preparing several dishes for a special meal, it can be assembled in advance and I can work on the other dishes while it is in the oven. Roasted potatoes or rice pilaf are nice accompaniments. If you have leftover pork, slice it and use it to make sandwiches with arugula, grilled red onions, and Peach Day Pickles (page 62).

Marcy

1¼ cups water

3 ounces home-dried peach slices (page 153), or 6 ounces store-bought dried peaches

1 (2½-pound) boneless pork loin
Coarse salt and freshly ground pepper

2 pinches of ground cloves

1 tablespoon all-purpose flour

½ cup Peach Jam (page 137)

2 tablespoons light brown sugar

1 tablespoon freshly squeezed lemon juice

Preheat the oven to 450°F.

Bring 1 cup of the water to a boil in a small saucepan. Coarsely chop the peaches, add them to the boiling water, and remove the pan from the heat. Let stand for 20 minutes. Using a slotted spoon, remove the peaches from the liquid, pressing against them to release the excess liquid back into the pan. Reserve the peaches and the liquid separately.

Trim the excess fat and silver skin from the loin, or ask your butcher to do this for you. Cut the pork loin into a ¾-inch-thick flat rectangle. Using a sharp knife and starting at one long side, make a lengthwise cut through the side of the loin to cut it open like a jelly roll, unrolling the meat until it is flat (as shown in photos 1 to 4 below). If needed, pound the meat

{CONTINUED}

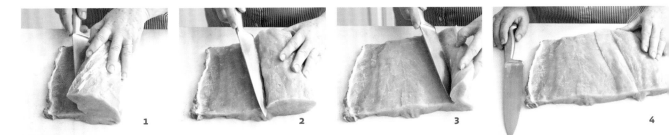

1   2   3   4

{CONTINUED FROM PAGE 83}

5

6

7

8

with a meat mallet to an even the thickness, then lay it flat on the work surface.

Lightly season the top surface of the meat with salt, pepper, and 1 pinch of the cloves. Spread the drained peaches evenly over the seasonings, leaving a 1-inch border on both short ends of the meat (as shown in photo 5). Starting at a short end, roll up the meat (like a jelly roll) to enclose the filling (as shown in photos 6 to 7). Tie the rolled meat with kitchen twine, encircling the meat every inch or so to ensure the roll holds it shape and the peach filling stays securely inside (as shown in photo 8). Place the tied roll, seam side down, in a roasting pan. (You do not need to use a meat rack.) In a small bowl, stir together the flour, the remaining pinch of cloves, and some salt and pepper. Sprinkle the top of the rolled pork with the flour mixture.

Place the pork in the oven and roast for 20 minutes. Lower the oven temperature to 350°F and continue to roast for about 25 minutes longer, until an instant-read thermometer inserted into the center of the roast registers 138°F.

While the meat is in the oven, add the jam and sugar to the soaking liquid remaining in the saucepan and bring to boil over medium-low heat, stirring to dissolve the sugar. Lower the heat to a simmer and cook, stirring occasionally, until the mixture is reduced to a slightly thick glaze.

When the meat registers 138°F (or after the 25 minutes), remove the roast from the oven and brush it with some of the glaze. Return the roast to the oven and continue to roast for 5 more minutes. The meat is done when the thermometer inserted into the center of the roast registers 145°F. If you don't have a meat thermometer, the meat should be golden on top, firm to the touch, and should not release pink juices when pierced with a knife.

Remove the roast from the oven, transfer to a cutting board, and reserve the juices in the pan. Tent the roast with aluminum foil and let rest for 10 minutes, then brush with the glaze again.

Make the sauce while the roast rests. Place the roasting pan over medium-high heat, add the remaining 1/4 cup water, bring to a simmer, and scrape the pan bottom to loosen the browned bits. Strain the contents of the pan through a fine-mesh sieve and add to the glaze remaining in the saucepan. Bring the sauce to a boil and simmer for 1 minute. Stir in the lemon juice.

Snip the twine on the pork roast, cut the roast into 1-inch-thick slices, and arrange on a warmed platter or individual plates. Serve with the sauce either on the side or spooned over the top.

CHAPTER FOUR

Sweet Dreams
SWEET DISHES and PEACH PLEASURE

"Life's a peach—enjoy each bite."

—MARCY

Losing Your Peach Virginity / BY MAS

PEOPLE OFTEN CELEBRATE FIRSTS, the first time we experience something, an initial moment that changes us, the starting point between what was and what will be different for the rest of our lives. Simultaneously, when we lose something—an innocence and naïveté—we also gain something: an experience and awakening. For our family, when we lost our peach virginity we discovered peaches meant something beyond just eating.

● ● ●

I was rather heavy as a child, kinda fat; "husky" jeans fit my body. I enjoyed eating. Every summer I loved to gorge myself on our best fruits.

Every day in our farm's packing shed, I did the simple chores a ten-year-old could do (mainly stamping our farm name on the wooden boxes). That summer, I began my hunt for the perfect peach: overripe and very soft. One day, I set a couple aside (demonstrating amazing patience for a kid) and kept searching for the right one.

By the late afternoon, I had chosen my champion. My mouth watered in anticipation, I held the huge treasure in my small hands and lifted it to my face. An animal-like urge compelled me to take a much too big first bite.

I remembered the sequence: teeth broke through the skin, juices squirted out, splashing the cheeks and an occasional bystander. The red fluids then painted my face and gathered on my chin before dripping. My white T-shirt collected my peach drool, especially where my robust tummy stuck out. All my shirts that summer had the same peach stain, a badge of honor for a farm kid growing up around perfect peaches.

● ● ●

When Nikiko, our daughter, was thirteen, we followed our peaches to market. At home, we had packed and shipped a small quantity of the best of the best to some of the finest restaurants in the state. Nikiko was confused by our fanatical quality standards. She knew most of our fruits were very good, but why the fuss about greatness?

We then visited one of these restaurants, and in its kitchen, we met the staff and watched them prep for that evening meal. Nikiko witnessed something we could never convey. A single peach was placed, stem side down, in the center of a white plate. Just before serving, the pastry chef would add a quick drizzle of color, like a raspberry swirl. Nikiko's peach stood alone, the single focus of this dessert. Uncomplicated. Elegant. Amazing.

Nikiko now understood that perfection could be found in the simple. She'd never look at another peach the same.

· · ·

When Marcy first came to the farm during the summer harvest, I hoped to impress her with our peaches. It worked too well. She loved the fruit but was initially shocked to see how much we had to cull: some were bruised, too soft, scarred, misshapen, or small. Her strong, frugal Wisconsin German genes kicked in: you can't waste this fruit!

She wasn't used to the rigors of a commercial orchard and the reality that not all of the fruits will make it to market. So she started a crusade to save them—all of them. She canned, jammed, and froze. She spent hours over the stove making chutney and sauces, syrups and soups, and anything else she could think of. She cooked, baked, and grilled throughout the summer. She dried and pickled peaches. She experimented so much she forgot to label some jars, and later in the year we had mystery peach something. She spent evenings with them instead of me. They were her babies.

She was introduced to a family peach farm and we were introduced to her. Single-handedly, she launched her own fuzz-to-pit-nose-to-tail-save-the-whole-peach movement. Today, I think we might still have an old jar of mystery peaches from those early days. Up high on a shelf in the basement pantry, her passion for all things peaches still sits from that inaugural summer, hidden but not forgotten.

· · ·

Korio was nine when he became a true peach veteran. He was a small guy, under four feet and a scant fifty pounds. But he loved to eat the biggest peaches he could wrap his little hands around. During that hot summer day, he held a huge peach with both hands. Most of his face was hidden behind that monster. He didn't lean over; instead the juices squirted over his face, his flesh was smeared with the meat, his cheeks glistened with peach pulp.

Then the half-eaten peach slipped out of his slick hands and rolled in the fine dust of the barnyard. Unfazed, he picked up the fallen fruit and returned to his binge, the earth adding a new texture. He was consumed by the consuming.

Later, when he lowered the fruit and grinned, our old farm dog Jake, an aging golden retriever, pulled himself up from sunning, moseyed over to the boy, and proceeded to lick clean the sticky face with long, even strokes. Korio closed his eyes during the tongue bath, a proper conclusion to his amazing peach feast.

My grandmother taught me how to eat a peach. She'd peel an overripe gem with a small knife, creating a dangling ribbon of skin as she rotated the fruit in her callused hand.

Sometimes she would stop, look up, and glance around to check if anyone was looking. Then she'd sneak a slice of the golden flesh and slip it into her mouth. She would close eyes and a gentle grin would grow across her face. She wore a look of comfort, a glow as she savored the taste.

When she opened her eyes and saw me, she smiled and offered me a slice. I shared a perfect moment with my grandmother. Closing my eyes, licking my lips, I too lost myself in the flavor I wanted to last forever.

So when did you lose your peach virginity?

MULTIGRAIN WAFFLES with SAUTÉED PEACHES

SERVES 3 OR 4

Sautéed peaches over your favorite breakfast carbs just might be the perfect dish to start your day. Our tree adoption families have enjoyed sautéed peaches over pancakes and French toast at brunches in our orchard on harvest day. We have also served this dish to Alice Waters, the Mother of California Cuisine, on our front porch. Anticipation of cooking for Alice got me the most anxious I can ever remember, but the stress was relieved by her warm smile and nod of approval when she sat back, satisfied from the meal. We often eat sautéed peaches over waffles or crepes when we take a midmorning break from packing peaches during harvest season. These multigrain waffles are delicious topped with just the peaches, but you can add a dollop of whipped cream, a few fresh mint leaves, a scattering of toasted nuts, and/or grated lemon zest, if you like.

Marcy

WAFFLES

- 3 eggs
- 1 1/2 cups milk
- 2 tablespoons plain yogurt
- 1/4 cup canola oil
- 1 teaspoon pure vanilla extract
- 1 cup unbleached all-purpose flour
- 1/2 cup whole wheat flour
- 1/2 cup rye flour
- 1 teaspoon baking powder
- 1/2 teaspoon baking soda
- 1/2 teaspoon salt
- 1/4 teaspoon ground cinnamon
- 1/4 cup almonds, pecans, or walnuts, coarsely chopped (optional)

Preheat the waffle iron. To make the waffle batter, in a large bowl, whisk together the eggs, milk, yogurt, oil, and vanilla. In a separate medium bowl, stir together the flours, baking powder, baking soda, salt, and cinnamon. Pour the dry ingredients into the wet ingredients and stir until well mixed but not overbeaten. Add the nuts and stir just to distribute evenly.

Brush the waffle iron grids with canola oil or use a natural cooking spray to coat your waffle iron. Following the manufacturer's instructions, spoon the batter onto the bottom grid of the waffle iron, close the iron, and cook as directed. When the waffle is ready, remove the waffle and keep warm. Repeat with the remaining batter.

SAUTÉED PEACHES

2   tablespoons salted or unsalted
    butter

3   large soft peaches, peeled, halved,
    pitted, and cut into 3/4-inch-wide
    wedges

1 1/2   teaspoons freshly squeezed lemon
        juice

1   to 3 tablespoons light brown sugar

1/4   teaspoon ground cinnamon

1   tablespoon brandy or other favorite
    spirit (optional)

    Pinch of salt (optional)

While the waffles are baking, make the sautéed peaches. Melt the butter in a large skillet over medium heat. Add the peaches and sauté until heated thorough but not yet cooked. You will notice that natural juices will form in the cooking process. Add the lemon juice, brown sugar to taste (depending on sweetness of peaches), cinnamon, and brandy and stir lightly until the flavorings are well blended. If your butter is unsalted, add the salt.

Serve the waffles with the peaches spooned over the top.

THINGS CAN GO WRONG • By Mas

Being in control is an approach to farming that I foolishly sought. When I first came back to the farm armed with a few years of experience, I began to believe I could dictate what would happen in our orchards. I made a calendar of the year's work—strategic planning at its best. But a business plan doesn't always include late-spring downpours and tractors breaking down. I had the illusion of being in control and was humbled when it reached 100°F in April. The trees responded well. I did not. My plans were changed forever.

I shudder at all the things that can go wrong when growing a peach. I used to try to keep precise data on farmwork: when blossoms arrived, the first day of harvest, the size and volume of the crop. I could see trends but little could be predicted. I had forgotten how beautiful the delicate blossoms are and how grateful I need to be for a single juicy, sweet peach. Humility is too easily lost in all the business of farming.

STUFFED FRENCH TOAST

SERVES 2 TO 4

Goat cheese and peach jam combine forces with the true star of this recipe: clarified butter. We are indebted to friend and cooking mentor Jim Dodge, who first introduced us to clarifying butter while helping us prepare a French toast brunch for serving in the orchard. The term *clarified butter* sounds more formidable than making it is: it's really just melted butter with its milk solids removed. It has a higher smoking point than regular butter and is thus wonderful for frying things like French toast. Cooking with clarified butter has been a total revelation for us. It makes the toast crisp on the outside, a perfect texture for dusting with confectioners' sugar or topping with maple syrup or peach jam.

Nikiko

4 slices French bread, 1 inch thick

STUFFING

1 teaspoon grated lemon zest

1 teaspoon grated orange zest

2 ounces fresh goat cheese

1/2 cup Peach Jam (page 137)

BATTER

2 eggs

1/2 cup milk

1 tablespoon clarified butter (see note, page 96)

Confectioners' sugar, maple syrup, or more jam, for serving

Using a small, sharp knife, cut each slice of bread horizontally almost in half, leaving just enough bread attached on the opposite side so that the slice opens flat like a book. The easiest way to do this is to place the slice on a flat surface, hold the knife level with the work surface, and press gently on the top of the slice with your other hand. As you cut, be careful not to tear any holes in the top or bottom of the slice.

To make the stuffing, in a small bowl, mash or stir both citrus zests with the goat cheese, mixing well. If the cheese is crumbly and not easy to spread, warm slightly in a microwave oven (about 10 seconds). Using a knife, spread one-fourth of the cheese-zest mixture on one of the internal sides of 1 bread slice, leaving the slice open. Now spread 2 tablespoons of the jam as evenly as possible on the other internal side of the slice. (When the cheese and jam are spread on opposite sides, they create a nice conversation of flavors, as opposed to a monologue.) Bring the halves together to close the slice. Repeat with the remaining bread slices and stuffing ingredients.

{CONTINUED}

{CONTINUED FROM PAGE 95}

To make the batter, beat together the eggs and milk in a bowl. Pour the batter into a pie plate or similarly shaped dish. Place the stuffed slices in the batter and let soak for 2 to 3 minutes. Flip the slices and let soak for 2 to 3 minutes longer, until all of the batter is soaked up.

Heat a large skillet over medium-high heat and add 1 tablespoon clarified butter. When the butter is hot, carefully place all the slices in the pan and cook for 3 to 4 minutes, until nicely colored on the first side. Turn the slices and cook for 3 to 4 minutes, until nicely colored on the second side.

Transfer to individual plates and let cool slightly before dusting with confectioners' sugar or topping with a little syrup or jam.

Cook's Note: To make clarified butter, heat any amount of unsalted butter in a heavy skillet or saucepan over low heat. (I recommend using at least 1/2 cup butter for efficiency's sake.) The butter will melt and begin to create foam. Keep cooking until the foam production (and popping sound) subsides. Do not let the butter color. Remove from the heat and skim off and discard the foam. Leaving the milk solids in the bottom of the pan, pour the remaining clarified butter into a clean bowl, let cool, cover, and refrigerate until needed.

Peaches have a dormant season. They need "chill hours," typically measured by winter hours below 45°F. We don't need freezing temperatures, just cold enough to keep trees asleep.

Usually our first cool nights come at the end of October. Autumn arrives, leaves change color, and trees slip into dormancy, dropping their leaves. Then, around the end of February and early March, they awaken with swelling buds and the first blooms. (Most peaches bloom before leaves push.)

Each peach variety needs a minimum number of chill hours to maintain its quality level. Older heirloom varieties often need more hours.

For example, Elbertas require about eight hundred hours. That means that from October to February, these trees need at least eight hundred hours of temperatures below 45°F. So if we have a good cold winter, our peaches should have a good bloom with lots of blossoms, excellent vegetative growth, and nice dense "meat." Too few chill hours make for grumpy fruit. It's as if they didn't get a good night's sleep, woke up cranky, and don't feel like going to work. No one likes grouchy peaches.

We want peaches that enjoyed a deep winter sleep so that they wake up in the spring refreshed. We want peaches that had sweet dreams.

PEACH SCONES

Our farmhouse was built almost a century ago, and it is not particularly well insulated. The kitchen is flanked by two huge windows that look out to our barn, some of our grapevines, and to trees. Even from inside, the farm is always part of our view. In the winter when the trees are bare, brown, and I'm eager for warm days to return, I bake to warm the house and my spirit. These scones, which call for dried peaches, bring a taste of summer into cold mornings. It's a lovely way to start a day during the off-season.

Nikiko

1	egg
1/2	cup milk, heavy cream, or half-and-half
2	ounces home-dried peaches (page 153) or store-bought dried peaches, cut into pieces about 1/4 inch square
1/2	cup whole wheat flour
1	cup unbleached all-purpose flour, plus more for working with the dough
2	teaspoons baking powder
1/2	teaspoon salt
1/3	cup sugar
6	tablespoons cold unsalted butter, cut into small chunks
	Peach Jam (page 137) and unsalted butter, for serving (optional)

Preheat the oven to 425°F. Have ready an ungreased baking sheet.

In a bowl, stir together the egg and milk until well mixed, then add the peaches. Let stand while preparing the other ingredients so the peaches can rehydrate.

In a bowl, stir together the flours, baking powder, salt, and sugar. Scatter the butter over the dry ingredients, then, with your fingers work the butter into the dry ingredients until the mixture has the texture of heavy sand. (Alternatively, combine flour mixture and butter in a food processor and pulse until mixture resembles heavy sand.)

Add the egg mixture to the dry ingredients and mix with your hands until a dough forms, scraping any moist bits from the sides and bottom of the bowl. Shape the dough into a large ball. Flour a work surface and transfer the dough to the floured surface. With floured hands, pat the dough into a disk about 8 inches in diameter and 1/2 inch thick. Cut the disk into 12 equal wedges and transfer them to the baking sheet.

Bake for 13 to 15 minutes, until the scones are lightly browned on the bottom. Serve warm with butter and peach jam.

WALNUT-PEACH STRUDEL

 SERVES 6 TO 8

Strudel reminds me of the stollen my mom would make for Christmas morning. She would roll all types of dried fruits, nuts, and candied citron into a light yeast dough. While I love stollen, I often don't have time to work with a leavened dough, so I prefer strudel. In honor of our local Greek American and Armenian American friends, I use phyllo dough for this strudel. You will find it in the frozen-food section at your supermarket or in Greek or Middle Eastern specialty stores. Several brands are available, and the sheet size varies with the brand. Depending on which brand you select, you may need to cut the sheets in half. You can repackage and refreeze the excess dough and use it for other recipes, such as Orange-Peach Phyllo Cups (page 103). I use raisins and dried peaches from our farm, but you may use homemade or store-bought dried peaches or other types of dried fruits, such as apricots, pears, nectarines, cherries, or cranberries.

Marcy

FRUIT FILLING

1¹/₂ cups peeled and diced fresh peaches with give (about ¹/₂ inch thick), or partially thawed frozen peaches (page 148)

2 teaspoons freshly squeezed lemon juice

¹/₂ teaspoon grated lemon zest

1 tablespoon granulated sugar

1 tablespoon all-purpose flour

¹/₄ teaspoon ground cinnamon
Pinch of ground allspice

¹/₄ cup raisins

¹/₄ cup chopped dried peaches, home dried (page 153) or store-bought

¹/₂ cup chopped walnuts

Preheat the oven to 350°F.

Place the sliced peaches in a bowl and drizzle with the lemon juice. In a separate small bowl, mix together the lemon zest, granulated sugar, flour, cinnamon, allspice, raisins, dried peaches, and walnuts. Pour the sugar-nut mixture over the peaches and mix gently, coating the peaches and evenly distributing the nuts. Let the mixture sit for about 5 minutes, until the sugar dissolves.

2 tablespoons firmly packed light brown sugar

2 tablespoons dried bread crumbs

1/2 cup unsalted butter, melted

10 sheets phyllo dough (about 9 by 12 inches), thawed according to package directions

Confectioners' sugar, for garnish

Meanwhile, in the now-empty small bowl, prepare the dry filling. Stir together the brown sugar and bread crumbs, breaking up the brown sugar and creating a light, crumbly mix. (You will notice that after you mix the packed brown sugar with the bread crumbs, the volume of the mixture expands to 6 tablespoons.)

This recipe makes 2 strudels, each of which uses 5 phyllo sheets. If you have not worked with phyllo, you will discover that you will need to work quickly and delicately because it is extremely thin and tears easily. Unwrap the thawed dough, place it on a sheet of plastic wrap, and cover it with a damp towel to keep it from drying out. As you remove each sheet from the stack, be sure to re-cover the remainder to prevent drying.

Lay a sheet of parchment paper slightly larger than a phyllo sheet (the dimensions are usually on the package) on a work surface. Lay 1 sheet of phyllo on the parchment. With a pastry brush, lightly coat the phyllo with the melted butter, being careful to brush all the way to the edges to ensure they don't dry out. Lay a second sheet on top of the first and brush again with butter to the edges. Sprinkle 1 tablespoon of the dry filling evenly over the second layer. Top with a third phyllo sheet and again brush with butter to the edges. Add a fourth phyllo sheet, brush with butter, and again sprinkle evenly with 1 tablespoon of the dry filling. Top with a fifth phyllo sheet, brush with butter, and sprinkle evenly with 1 tablespoon of the dry filling.

Position the rectangular phyllo stack with a long side facing you and the short sides to the right and left. About 2 inches from the long side closest to you, spoon half of the fruit filling horizontally across the dough in a log shape, leaving about 1 inch uncovered at both short side edges. Fold the uncovered short sides over the filling, like the sides of an envelope. Pick up the long side nearest you, fold it over the peach filling, and

{CONTINUED}

{CONTINUED FROM PAGE 101}

gently roll to the far long edge (much like rolling up an egg roll or burrito). Place a second sheet of parchment paper on a baking sheet. Gently transfer the roll, seam side down, to one side of the parchment-lined pan. To make air vents, using a sharp knife, cut 4 or 5 diagonal slits across the roll, making them 1 to 2 inches long and spacing them about 1 inch apart. The slits should just pierce the top of the roll. They must not be too big or the filling will push through them as it cooks.

Using the remaining phyllo sheets and fillings, make a second strudel in the same manner. (You may need to reheat the butter to keep it from solidifying.) Place the second roll, seam side down, on the pan, spacing the rolls at least 1 to 2 inches apart. If you have any butter and/or dry filling left over, brush the tops of the rolls with the butter and sprinkle with any remaining filling.

Bake the strudels for 35 to 40 minutes, until golden. Let cool to room temperature before cutting. Dust with the confectioners' sugar before serving.

Cook's Note: If the strudel picks up moisture and the pastry is not crispy when it's time to eat, place it on a baking sheet in a 350°F oven for 10 minutes. The pastry will crisp up nicely.

ORANGE-PEACH PHYLLO CUPS

As noted in the introduction to Walnut-Peach Strudel (page 100), packages of phyllo sheets are usually found in the frozen-food section of supermarkets, and any unused sheets can be refrozen for months or saved in the refrigerator for three weeks. Last winter, I was looking for a way to use some extra phyllo dough I had in the freezer at the same time that I had oranges from our backyard tree. So, in essence, my practical and frugal nature is what birthed this recipe. I hope you enjoy the combination of orange, peach, yogurt, and phyllo as much as we do.

Marcy

1 1/2 tablespoons unsalted butter, melted and cooled

2 to 6 sheets phyllo dough (depending on the size in your package), thawed according to package directions, and cut into 6 (6-inch) squares

1 cup peeled and sliced fresh peaches (1/2-inch thick), or frozen (page 148)

1 to 2 oranges, peeled and sectioned to make 1 cup, reserving any juice, the peels, and any pulp

2 tablespoons Peach Jam (page 137)

1 (3-inch) cinnamon stick

1 (3-inch) piece vanilla bean

6 tablespoons vanilla yogurt

Fresh mint leaves, for garnish

Preheat the oven to 350°F. With a pastry brush, lightly butter 6 ramekins, each 3 inches in diameter and 1 to 1 1/2 inches deep, or 6 cups in a standard muffin pan, alternating holes to allow room for the phyllo squares to drape over the edges and not touch one another. Set the buttered molds aside.

If you have not worked with phyllo, you will discover that you will need to work quickly and delicately because it is extremely thin and tears easily. Unwrap the thawed dough, place it on a sheet of plastic wrap, and cover it with a damp towel to keep it from drying out. As you remove each sheet from the stack, be sure to re-cover the remainder to prevent drying.

Lay a sheet of parchment paper slightly larger than a phyllo sheet (the dimensions are usually on the box) on a work surface. Lay 1 sheet of phyllo on the parchment. With a pastry brush, lightly coat the phyllo with the butter, being careful to brush all the way to the edges to ensure they don't dry out. Lay a second sheet of phyllo over the first, and brush with melted butter. Cut the stacked sheets into squares each measuring roughly 6 by 6 inches.

{CONTINUED}

{CONTINUED FROM PAGE 103}

Working quickly so that the dough does not dry out, crack, or tear, center the stacked squares buttered sides up over a buttered ramekin or muffin-pan cup, gently push the center down into the hole to form a cup shape, and leave the edges of the dough draped over the rim in a free-form manner. Repeat with the remaining phyllo sheets until you have lined all 6 molds.

If you are using ramekins, place them on a baking sheet for ease of moving them in and out of the oven. Bake the phyllo cups for 8 to 12 minutes, until golden throughout. Remove from oven and set aside to cool. I have noticed that the phyllo cups in the muffin pan bake much faster than those in the ramekins.

While the phyllo cups are baking, place the peach slices and orange sections and any reserved juice in a saucepan, then squeeze the reserved orange peels and pulp to release any additional juice into the pan. Add the jam and cinnamon stick, then slit the vanilla bean lengthwise to expose the seeds and add to the pan as well. Place over medium heat and bring to a boil, stirring gently until the jam liquefies and being careful not to break up the orange sections. Reduce the heat to medium-low and cook the fruits for 2 to 3 minutes.

Using a slotted spoon, remove the fruits from the syrup and place in a small bowl to cool. Do not remove the cinnamon stick and vanilla bean yet. Continue cooking the syrup over medium-low heat for 5 to 10 minutes, until the syrup reduces by one-half. Remove the syrup from the heat and let cool. Remove the cinnamon stick and vanilla bean.

To serve, carefully remove the cooled phyllo cups from their molds and put them on individual dessert plates. Put 1 table-spoon of the yogurt in the bottom of each cup. Layer the cooled peaches and oranges on top of the yogurt, dividing them evenly. Top the fruit in each cup with $1^1/_2$ teaspoons of the syrup. Garnish with the mint and serve.

PEACH SHORTCAKE

I didn't have a perfect relationship with my German American grandmother. We never really developed comfortable or open channels of communication, and even if we had, I know many of our opinions would have clashed. Despite our vast differences and silences, I have come to realize that I inherited a lot of recipes and kitchen knowledge indirectly from her through my mom. My love of shortcake is one of them. I ate my first homemade shortcake at my grandma's house. I remember loving the hearty biscuit-style cake that contrasted perfectly with the sweet strawberries. My version of peach shortcake follows in this tradition: the biscuit is more sub stantive than it is sweet, which provides the perfect excuse for eating this shortcake for breakfast or dessert. I suppose that there are some things that we inherit without knowing it. I am grateful for how my grandmother's cooking wisdom remains in my life.

Nikiko

SHORTCAKES

2 1/2 cups unbleached all-purpose flour, plus more for working with the dough

1 tablespoon granulated sugar

1 tablespoon baking powder

3/4 teaspoon salt

1/2 cup cold unsalted butter, cut into small chunks

1 cup milk

WHIPPED CREAM

1/2 cup heavy cream

1 1/2 teaspoons confectioners' sugar

1/2 teaspoon pure vanilla extract

2 soft or gushy peaches

Scant 1/2 teaspoon freshly squeezed lemon juice

Sugar, for sweetening (optional)

Preheat the oven to 425°F. Have ready an ungreased baking sheet.

To make the shortcakes, in a large bowl, stir together the flour, sugar, baking powder, and salt. Scatter the butter over the top. Using your fingers, work the butter into the dry ingredients until the mixture resembles little pebbles or sand. (Alternatively, combine the dry ingredients in a food processor and pulse to mix. Scatter the butter over the top and pulse until the mixture resembles little pebbles or sand, then transfer to a bowl.) Add the milk and mix with a few strokes of a fork or wooden spoon just until combined.

With floured hands, gather the dough into a ball; it will be very sticky. Generously dust a work surface with flour and place the dough on the floured surface. Roll out the dough into a round about 1/2 inch thick. Using a round biscuit cutter or the rim of a glass, cut out 3-inch rounds. Repeat the process, gathering the scraps and rerolling into one or two more rounds. Transfer the rounds to the baking sheet.

{CONTINUED}

{CONTINUED FROM PAGE 107}

Bake the shortcakes for 15 to 17 minutes, until the bottoms are browned and the tops spring back when touched lightly. Let cool completely on the pan on a wire rack.

To make the whipped cream, pour the cream into a bowl and add the sugar and vanilla. Beat with an electric mixer (or by hand with a whisk) until soft, airy peaks form. Cover and refrigerate for up to 2 hours.

Peel, halve, and pit the peaches and cut into bite-size pieces. Place in a bowl, sprinkle with the lemon juice, and toss to coat evenly. (The lemon juice prevents the peaches from turning brown.) If the peaches are not sweet enough, sprinkle with a little sugar and toss to mix.

To serve, using a knife or fork, split the shortcakes in half horizontally. Place the bottom halves, cut side up, on individual plates. Spoon a heaping serving of peaches over each one and top with a dollop of whipped cream. Close with the top halves and serve.

PEACH-DATE BARS

MAKES 9 TO 12 BARS

These are three-layer bars, similar to an old-fashioned apricot bar my mother used to make. When we were kids, my brother, sister, and I would fight over who got the last one, which was always in less than 24 hours after they were out of the oven. I was the youngest and the chubbiest sibling, so I wonder who won? Somehow, I don't remember!

Marcy

TOP AND BOTTOM LAYERS

- 1/2 cup unsalted butter, at room temperature
- 2/3 cup firmly packed light brown sugar
- 1 cup plus 1 tablespoon unbleached all-purpose flour
- Scant 1/2 teaspoon baking soda
- 1/2 teaspoon salt
- 1 cup rolled oats, preferably old-fashioned

FILLING

- 1 1/3 cups chopped dates
- 2 1/2 cups peeled and chopped, mashed, or pureed soft or gushy peaches
- 1/4 cup granulated sugar
- 2 tablespoons freshly squeezed lemon juice

Preheat the oven to 400°F. Have ready a 9-inch square baking dish.

To make the top and bottom layers, in a bowl, using an electric mixer, beat together the butter and brown sugar on low to medium speed until smooth and fluffy. In a second bowl, sift together the flour, baking soda, and salt. Add the flour mixture to the butter mixture and beat until fully combined. Add the oats and beat on low speed until mixed and crumbly. Press half of the mixture into the bottom of the baking dish. Reserve the remaining half of the mixture for the top layer.

To make the filling, in a saucepan, combine the dates, peaches, granulated sugar, and lemon juice, place over medium heat, and bring to a boil, stirring to prevent the bottom from scorching. Continue boiling for about 2 minutes, stirring constantly. Remove from the heat.

Spread the hot filling over the bottom layer. Sprinkle the reserved oat mixture evenly over the filling, then lightly press to firm the crumbles on top.

Bake for 30 to 35 minutes, until the topping is golden brown. Let cool completely on a wire rack. Cut into 9 to 12 bars to serve.

Cook's Note: If you don't have fresh peaches, use 2 1/2 cups Peach Jam (page 137) in place of the peaches and sugar.

PEACH GALETTE

MAKES ONE 8 TO 9-INCH GALETTE; SERVES 6 TO 8

If I were making dessert for one of my favorite movie stars, George Clooney or Meryl Streep, I'd bake this galette because it is simple, rustic, and honest. If you want to serve it to a large group for a special gathering, the recipe doubles easily to make a 12-inch galette. Accompany with a dollop of whipped cream or vanilla ice cream and you have a totally scrumptious home-style dessert.

Marcy

PASTRY

- 3/4 cup unbleached all-purpose flour, plus more for working with the dough
- 6 tablespoons whole wheat flour
- 1 tablespoon granulated sugar
  Scant 1/2 teaspoon kosher salt
- 1/2 cup plus 1 tablespoon cold unsalted butter, cut into small chunks
- 1 large egg
- 1 1/2 teaspoons milk
- 1 tablespoon beaten egg or heavy cream
  Turbinado sugar, for sprinkling

FILLING

- 1/2 cup granulated sugar
- 3 tablespoons unbleached all-purpose flour or tapioca flour
- 1/2 teaspoon ground cinnamon
- 6 to 8 soft peaches or with give, peeled, halved, pitted, and cut into 1/4 to 1/2-inch-thick wedges

To make the pastry, combine the flours, granulated sugar, and salt in a food processor and pulse until blended. Scatter the butter over the flour mixture and pulse until it looks like coarse sand. (Alternatively, combine the flour, sugar, and salt in a bowl and work the mixture with a pastry blender until it has a sand-like texture.) In a small bowl or cup, whisk together the 1 egg and the milk until blended, pour into the food processor or bowl all at once, and pulse or gently mix by hand until the dough forms a rough clump. Do not overwork the dough to avoid toughness.

Lightly flour a work surface. Transfer the dough to the floured surface, form it into a ball, and then flatten into a disk 1 to 1 1/2 inches thick. Don't knead it! Wrap it in plastic wrap and refrigerate for at least 1 1/2 to 2 hours or for up to 1 day.

When the dough is well chilled, preheat the oven to 375°F.

Remove the dough from the refrigerator and let it warm at room temperature for about 10 minutes. Meanwhile, make the filling. In a small bowl, stir together the granulated sugar, the flour, and the cinnamon, mixing well. Place the peaches in a bowl, sprinkle the sugar mixture over the top, and toss gently. (If the peaches are tart, you may want to add a little more sugar.)

{CONTINUED}

{CONTINUED FROM PAGE 111}

Lay a large sheet of parchment paper on a work surface and dust the parchment with flour. Place the dough on the floured parchment and roll it out into a round about 11 inches in diameter and 1/8 inch thick. Transfer the pastry with the parchment to a rimmed or rimless baking sheet large enough to accommodate the pastry round comfortably. Starting 1 to 1 1/2 inches from the edge of the round, arrange the peach wedges in a single layer in concentric circles, continuing until you reach the center of the round. Fold the outer edges of the pastry over the peaches, creating overlapping folds as you work around the perimeter. If your peaches are extra juicy, leave the extra juice in the bowl so that the filling does not overflow in the oven. Brush the pastry border with 1 tablespoon beaten egg and then sprinkle lightly with the turbinado sugar.

Bake for 50 to 60 minutes, until the crust is golden and the filling is bubbling. If your galette has a lot of juice, you may want to place a second pan on the lowest rack in the oven under the baking sheet to catch any juices that overflow.

Let the galette cool on the baking sheet on a wire rack. Cut into wedges to serve.

BONUS GRATIFICATION • By Mas

We first gave bonuses to our workers a few years ago, a gift for their hard work. It had been too long before we realized they deserved to be acknowledged. But I was embarrassed: I didn't know the word *bonus* in Spanish. I asked our workers, but they didn't know, either. None of them had ever received one. Finally, one crew boss offered his word, *gratificación*. It fit the act well.

I try to value these hands that help grow our peaches. We try to create good working conditions. Farming organically helps avoid any pesticide poisoning issues. We offer steady work as best we can for a small operation. And we do pay modest bonuses. It's not much but appreciated. We, too, are grateful.

PEACH CROSTATA

This dessert, made in a 9-inch tart pan, is both easy and beautiful. The tart pan gives it a professional look that seems to impress people. The crust is cookie-like and very light and is a sweet contrast to the peaches. I have made this dessert for family and friends numerous times and have always had great compliments.

Marcy

PASTRY

- 1¼ cups unbleached all-purpose flour
- ⅓ cup sugar
- ¼ teaspoon salt
- ½ cup cold unsalted butter, cut into ¼-inch cubes
- 1 egg yolk

FILLING

- ½ cup sugar
- 3 tablespoons unbleached flour or tapioca flour
- 5 or 6 peaches with give, peeled, halved, pitted, and cut into ¼ to ½-inch-thick slices
- 3 tablespoons Peach Jam (page 137) or apricot jam, if the peaches are tart
  Ground cinnamon

  Vanilla bean ice cream or whipped cream, for serving

Preheat the oven to 375°F.

To make the pastry, combine the flour, sugar, salt, and butter in a food processor and pulse until the mixture has the texture of coarse sand. Add the egg yolk and continue to pulse until evenly combined. The dough will be crumbly and quite dry. (Alternatively, combine the flour, sugar, salt, and butter in a bowl and work the mixture with a pastry blender until crumbly. Add the egg and mix until evenly combined.) Transfer the crumbles to a 9-inch tart pan with a removable bottom. Pat the crust firmly and evenly across the bottom and up the sides of the pan.

To make the filling, in a small bowl, stir together the sugar and flour, mixing well. Place the peaches in a separate bowl, sprinkle the sugar mixture over the top, and toss gently. Arrange the peach slices in a single layer in an attractive manner on the tart shell. If the peaches are on the ripe side, juices will have built up in the bowl. Pour these sweet juices over the arranged peaches. If the peaches are tart and relatively firm, not much sweet juice will have developed, in which case you will need to use the jam. Heat it in a microwave for several seconds (or over low heat on the stove top) and then brush it over the arranged peach slices. Sprinkle the peaches lightly with cinnamon.

{CONTINUED}

{CONTINUED FROM PAGE 113}

Place the tart pan on a baking sheet or other pan to collect juices that may overflow. Bake for about 50 minutes, until the crust and peaches are golden and the peach juices are bubbling. Let the *crostata* cool to room temperature on a wire rack. The filling will solidify as it cools.

Remove the ring from the pan bottom and cut the *crostata* into wedges. Divide among individual plates and accompany with the ice cream.

BLACKBERRY-PEACH BREAD PUDDING

MAKES ONE 9-INCH SQUARE PUDDING; SERVES 6 TO 9

When I was a kid, my mom used to make bread pudding as a wintertime comfort food. The only fruit she used in it were raisins. I have since modified the concept, replacing the raisins with peaches and berries. You can substitute nectarines for the peaches, and raspberries, boysenberries, or blueberries for the blackberries, but I like it best with peaches and blackberries. To increase the nutritional value, I use half regular French and half whole wheat French bread. Save the rest of the French bread for Stuffed French Toast (page 95). Or, you can increase the recipe by 50 percent, using a whole loaf and a 9 by 13-inch baking pan. Some people serve a sweet caramel sauce (or a bourbon sauce if you're from New Orleans!) with their bread pudding, but I like it without the extra calories and sugar. If you crave a sauce, you might try it with the raspberry sauce that accompanies Peach Melba (page 127).

We have made this for brunch for our Elberta peach adoption participants, and it was well received by the crowd. Two of the best things about it is that you can prepare it ahead of time and you can serve it as a brunch main dish or as a dessert.

Marcy

2/3 loaf stale French bread or whole wheat French bread, cut or torn into 3/4-inch cubes (about 7 cups)

1 1/3 cups peeled and diced fresh peaches, soft or with give, or partially thawed frozen peaches (page 148)

2/3 cup fresh or frozen blackberries

Place the bread in a large bowl, scatter the peaches and berries over the top, and toss to distribute all the ingredients evenly. Transfer the mixture to a lightly greased 9 by 9-inch baking dish. Set aside.

2   tablespoons salted butter

2   cups milk

2   eggs

2/3   cup half-and-half

2/3   cup granulated sugar

1/2   cup firmly packed light brown sugar

1/2   teaspoon pure vanilla extract

1   tablespoon Grand Marnier (optional)
      Ground cinnamon, for sprinkling

In a saucepan, combine the butter and milk and heat over medium-low heat just until the butter melts. Do not allow the milk to boil.

While the milk and butter are heating, in a bowl, whisk together the eggs, half-and-half, both sugars, vanilla, and Grand Marnier. Slowly whisk the warmed milk mixture into the egg mixture to make a batter. Pour the batter evenly over the bread and fruit in the baking dish. Cover with plastic wrap and refrigerate for at least 1 hour or up to overnight.

When ready to bake, preheat the oven to 350°F.

Uncover the baking dish and lightly sprinkle the surface of the bread mixture with the cinnamon. Bake for about 55 minutes, until the pudding is puffy, the bread on top becomes golden, and the batter is set. When the bread pudding comes out of the oven, it should still wiggle if the dish is shaken but will set as it cools. Let the pudding rest for at least 30 minutes before serving.

Serve the pudding warm, at room temperature, or cold. Cut into squares to serve.

Peach Porn / BY MAS

I WRITE PEACH PORN. My writing has been accused of being syrupy and sentimental. Some critics claim my stories too often connect food fantasies with everyday eating: I romanticize the relationship between a farmer and a luscious, juicy peach. I never thought of the farm as an accidental porn star.

Have peaches become merely objects of desire, instruments of promotion, shaped by unrealistic expectations gleaned from an artificial creation? The evolution of this salacious star began decades ago. I witnessed the introduction of sexy lipstick red peaches that began to dominate the marketplace. My peaches with mixed hues of yellow-gold-red blush were blacklisted because they "lacked color."

Through the 1960s and 1970s, consumers were trained to shop with their eyes; suddenly only the visual mattered. Peaches submitted to an objectification, reduced to a commodity defined solely by appearance. Ultimately, people began to eat with their eyes: the redder the better and a new industry was born. Peaches experienced an extreme makeover. By the 1990s, images began to portray them as lush bodies of gratification, hero shots (the glossy, glamorous photos in food magazines and cookbooks) of an imaginary blemish-free treasure for the taking. Cooking with them produced gorgeous and immaculate dishes, at least in the pictures. The image became the reality, a type of magical mirage so perfect that it possibly couldn't be replicated. But that didn't matter. Looks did.

People lusted after this new perfect peach, and all peaches were not equally desirous. Some had the "it" factor and ours didn't. So we responded on our farm with equal passion. After all, we felt our peaches were authentic and real. We then found homes for them in the organic marketplace and progressive kitchens, joining a new, chic foodie revolution.

Have I become a newly fashioned peach pimp who, along with chefs, use peach desire for profit and power?

Or is this art? Peaches are expressions of my creative soul. If so, then I insist farmers be included in photo layouts. Our dirty stories of farming can also be sexy.

I lick my lips often during harvest, wanting to remind people that if they don't know real taste, how do they know what they're missing? Eating peaches should be a sensual experience, not a vicarious one: part of something real—so real that you can touch it and taste it with your mouth and tongue.

My goal is not to remove peaches from real life but the opposite. I want to include and not exclude remembrances of things past. Flavor with sweat. Delight with pain. Sweetness and Masumoto peaches, S&M on our farm?

I'm still guilty of peach porn, imagining highly charged and emotional moments of pleasure, a lapse of nostalgia I defend: the idealized working-class illusions help get me through the hard workdays. Am I not allowed to wax poetically? Promoting indulgence can be liberating for both the producer and the consumer.

Every day I cringe at the vast amounts of nonconsensual eating because the farmer is left out of the equation. We haven't given permission; external forces, such as the marketplace, dictate which produce becomes available for the consumer and who has access to food. Salability defines what is good. That means that peaches are picked when they are immature: they're too young and green so they arrive hard and firm, without bruises, and, in grocery parlance, with little shrink.

Have we reached a new phase of food porn? Now we farmers and others in the food industry have to dress up our produce in gourmet outfits. Peaches masquerade in unattainable bodies, a form of peach fakery that makes huge, bulbous mounds of flesh the new norm. Size matters.

On our farm, we lament when small, perky, cute peaches are left unharvested because there is no market for them. Today, the marketplace wants both glowing color and size in its insatiable hunger for perfection. We have created an unreal world of food. But to a public far removed from rural life, farming itself has become unreal.

As a farmer, I feel responsible for what people put into their bodies. As a writer, I hope to share authentic farm stories. During my grandparents' generation, the majority of Americans still lived in rural communities and understood where food came from. Of course, their food choices were limited: they didn't have to think so damned much with each mouthful. Folks didn't have to judge as much because they didn't have much.

The mass exodus from countryside to city happened quickly and absolutely, and now family farms are exotic places far removed from recent family histories. Such distance creates room for unabashed sentimentality and lack of critical thought. Complicated issues of social justice, the environment, and the harsh economics of farming are quickly lost in the alluring imagery of virgin orchards and peaches gently kissed by the morning dew. That attitude ends up trivializing everyone in the food chain, especially the farmer.

Do I hope for an idealized future in which farmers and foodies walk hand in hand? Yep, with farmers as the guides and interpreters. Ultimately, I can't separate peaches from our family identity, nor do I want to. This is about the self.

In the end, perhaps it's about the real and the imagined, the authentic and the contrived. Farmers have probably always blurred the lines. After all, we strive to manipulate nature simply by planting a seed. And cooks hope to create something greater as they combine individual ingredients. Isn't this all about dreaming of a transformative food moment?

Beyond the bright lights, I understand many just want to eat a good meal. Readers want writers they trust. And peach porn is better than no porn, I suppose. At least it got you looking at my peaches.

HEARTY PEACH COBBLER

This wholesome cobbler can double for breakfast or dessert in the Masumoto household. Because Mas has a sweet tooth and goes to bed long before I do during harvest season, I often bake this cobbler before going to bed, then leave it on the kitchen counter to cool. By the time I get up in the morning, he has usually already eaten a good portion of it! I almost always make it in a 9-by 13-inch baking dish because I have lots of peaches available. Just increase the recipe by 50 percent for a 9 by 13-inch baking dish.

Marcy

FILLING

- 6 to 7 cups peeled and diced soft or gushy peaches
- 2 tablespoons instant tapioca
- 1/4 to 1/3 cup granulated sugar
- 2 teaspoons freshly squeezed lemon juice
- 1/4 teaspoon kosher salt

TOPPING

- 2/3 cup rolled oats, preferably old-fashioned
- 2 1/2 tablespoons granulated sugar
- 3/4 teaspoon kosher salt
  Grated zest of 1/2 lemon
- 2/3 cup unbleached all-purpose flour
- 2 teaspoons baking powder
- 3 1/2 tablespoons cold unsalted butter, cut into 1/4-inch cubes
- 1/3 cup heavy cream
- 2 1/2 tablespoons buttermilk

- 1 to 2 teaspoons turbinado sugar (optional)

Preheat the oven to 400°F. Have ready a 9-inch square baking dish.

To make the filling, in a large bowl, combine the peaches, tapioca, granulated sugar, lemon juice, and salt, using the larger amount of sugar if your peaches aren't very sweet. Mix gently with a large spoon to combine the ingredients evenly. Pour the filling into the baking dish and set aside.

To make the topping, in a bowl, combine the oats, granulated sugar, salt, and lemon zest. Sift together the flour and baking powder, add to the oat mixture, and whisk to combine. Scatter the butter over the dry ingredients. Using a pastry blender or your fingers, work in the butter until it is the size of small peas. Add the cream and buttermilk and mix with a fork just until evenly moistened.

Drop 1/4 cup clumps of the topping on top of the peach filling, distributing them evenly. Sprinkle the clumps with the turbinado sugar.

Bake for 35 to 40 minutes, until the topping is golden and is baked all the way through (it should sound hollow when tapped with a spoon) and the peaches are bubbling. Remove from the oven and let cool completely. The filling will set as the cobbler cools. Serve at room temperature.

FRENCH PEACH COBBLER

The Gilbert girls, one of our peach-adopting families, shared this recipe with me. They originally found it in their mother's 1963 *McCall's Cook Book*, and I have modified it to fit our tastes. It's a light, simple cobbler that everyone seems to love. I've listed a range for the amount of sugar because the quantity depends on the sweetness of your peaches. If you have tart peaches, use the larger amount of sugar. If your peaches are very sweet, use the smaller amount or even less. If your peaches are dry, add 1/4 cup water. If they are juicy, omit the water. I *never* use water with ripe Masumoto peaches!

Marcy

FILLING

5 cups peeled and sliced peaches with give or frozen peaches

1/3 to 2/3 cup sugar

2 tablespoons unbleached all-purpose flour

1/2 teaspoon ground cinnamon

1/4 teaspoon salt

BATTER

1/2 cup unbleached all-purpose flour

1/3 cup sugar

1/2 teaspoon baking powder

1/4 teaspoon salt

2 tablespoons unsalted butter, at room temperature

1 egg, lightly beaten

1/4 teaspoon pure almond extract

Vanilla bean ice cream or softly whipped cream, for serving (optional)

Preheat the oven to 375°F. Have ready a 9-inch square baking dish.

To make the filling, in a bowl, combine the peaches, sugar, flour, cinnamon, and salt, using the larger amount of sugar if your peaches aren't very sweet. If the peaches are not juicy, add 1/4 cup water. Pour the filling into the baking pan.

To make the batter, in a bowl, combine the flour, sugar, baking powder, salt, butter, egg, and almond extract. Stir together with a wooden spoon or a rubber spatula until the batter is smooth.

Drop spoonfuls of the batter on top of the fruit, forming 9 spoonfuls in all and spacing them evenly over the fruit. The batter will be very thick but will spread during baking.

Bake for 40 to 45 minutes, until the fruit is tender and topping is golden and springs up after touching (you can test it as you would a cake). Remove from the oven and let cool before serving. The filling will set as the cobbler cools.

Serve warm or at room temperature, accompanied with the ice cream or whipped cream.

PEACH CRISP

I love crisps because they are so easy to make and delicious—like eating granola atop your favorite fruit filling! If your peaches are extremely juicy, drain the juice after cutting the peaches and reserve it to enjoy as a refreshing beverage when the crisp goes in the oven.

Marcy

TOPPING

1/4 cup pecans, almonds, or walnuts

1/2 cup unbleached all-purpose flour

2 tablespoons light brown sugar

2 tablespoons granulated sugar

1/4 teaspoon ground cinnamon

Pinch of salt

6 tablespoons cold unsalted butter, cut into 1/4-inch cubes

1/2 cup rolled oats, preferably old-fashioned

FILLING

1 1/2 tablespoons cornstarch, instant tapioca, or tapioca flour

1 tablespoon sugar

5 cups peeled and sliced soft peaches (3 to 4 pounds)

Heavy cream, warmed, for serving (optional)

Preheat oven to 350°F. Have ready a 9-inch square baking dish or 4 to 6 individual ramekins or tartlet pans.

To make the topping, spread the nuts in a small shallow pan and toast in the oven, stirring once or twice, for 10 to 15 minutes, until fragrant and golden. Pour onto a cutting board and let cool. Increase the oven temperature to 375°F.

Chop the cooled nuts. In a bowl, stir together the flour, both sugars, cinnamon, and salt. Scatter the butter over the dry ingredients. Using a pastry blender or your fingers, gently work in the butter until the mixture is crumbly. Stir in the rolled oats and nuts and set aside.

To make the filling, in a small bowl, stir together the cornstarch and sugar. Place the peaches in a large bowl, sprinkle the cornstarch mixture over the top, and toss gently. Pour the filling into the baking dish, ramekins, or tartlet pans. Sprinkle the topping evenly over the filling.

Bake for 35 to 40 minutes, until the topping is browned and bubbling is visible around the edges. Remove from the oven and let cool until at least warm before serving.

Serve warm or at room temperature. If you're up for a few additional calories and richness, pour the warm cream over each serving just before serving.

OLD-FASHIONED PEACH PIE

MAKES ONE 9-INCH DOUBLE-CRUST PIE; SERVES 6 TO 8

Peach pie is the first thing that comes to my mind when people ask me what my favorite peach dessert is. I think that's because I grew up in a pie-baking family. I really like to pile in the peaches and minimize the added sugar in the filling to attempt to improve the nutritive value of the pie. But in the end, I have come to realize that if you're going to eat pie, you shouldn't worry about its nutritional heft. Instead, just enjoy the pie!

My mom always used lard to make piecrust, never shortening, oil, or butter. That was back when I was a kid and we had homemade lard from the milk-fed pigs we raised and butchered for the family each year. I like the flavor of lard, but because I don't have access to homemade lard nowadays, I use a combination of butter and shortening. This recipe is for pastry for double-crust pie, but it can also be used for two 9-inch single crust pies. Just divide the dough ball in half, roll out the dough, line the pie pan, and trim the overhang as directed, then fold the overhang under to create a high edge on the pan rim and flute the edge attractively.

The tricky thing about peach pie is adjusting the amount of thickener (flour or tapioca) in relation to the juiciness of your peaches. Because our peaches are extremely juicy, which is how they are supposed to be, I always put aluminum foil or a pan on the rack below my pie to catch juices that might escape during baking. That saves a lot of time cleaning the oven! If you have extra-juicy peaches, you may want to do a lattice-top crust or cut larger holes in the top crust to allow more steam to vent. If your pie does not cool completely or has not baked long enough, the filling will be runny, so make sure you leave it in the oven long enough and let it cool fully to room temperature before cutting into it!

If you are using a deep-dish pie pan, use 7 to 8 cups sliced peaches and increase the sugar and flour or tapioca accordingly.

Marcy

PASTRY

- **3** cups unbleached all-purpose flour
- **1** tablespoon sugar
- **1¹/₂** teaspoons salt
- **¹/₂** cup cold unsalted butter, cut into ¹/₂-inch cubes
- **¹/₂** cup vegetable shortening (not margarine), chilled
- **6** to 7 tablespoons ice water

In a large bowl, stir together the flour, sugar, and salt, mixing well. Distribute the butter and shortening over the flour mixture. Using a pastry blender, work in the butter until it is the size of small peas. Add the water, 1 tablespoon at a time, and work it into the flour mixture with your hands until it is moist enough to hold together and you can shape it into a ball. Do not overwork the dough or the pastry will be tough.

{CONTINUED}

FILLING

6 cups peeled and sliced fresh peaches with give or partially thawed frozen peaches (page 148)

2 tablespoons freshly squeezed lemon juice

3/4 cup granulated sugar

3 to 4 tablespoons all-purpose flour, instant tapioca, or tapioca flour

1/4 teaspoon ground cinnamon
Pinch of salt

2 tablespoons cold salted butter, cut into 1/4-inch cubes

1 tablespoon heavy cream or half-and-half (optional)

1 teaspoon turbinado sugar (optional)

(Alternatively, combine the flour, sugar, and salt in a food processor and pulse to mix well. Distribute the butter and shortening over the flour mixture and pulse until the fat is the size of small peas. Add the water, 1 tablespoon at a time, and pulse until the mixture comes together in a rough mass. Remove the dough from the processor and shape into a ball.)

Divide the dough into 2 balls, one slightly larger than the other. Flatten each ball into a disk 1 to 1 1/2 inches thick. Wrap each disk in plastic wrap and refrigerate the disks for at least 1 hour or up to 2 days.

When you are ready to assemble the pie, dust your work surface with flour. Unwrap the larger disk, place on the floured surface, and roll out into a round at least 13 inches in diameter and 1/8 inch thick. Transfer the round to a 9-inch pie pan, gently fitting it into the bottom and sides. Trim the edge of the pastry to leave a 1-inch overhang around the rim of the pan.

Preheat the oven to 400°F.

Place the peaches in a large bowl. Drizzle them with the lemon juice and stir gently to coat evenly.

If your peaches are especially juicy, drain off the excess juice and reserve for drinking later—or even while you make the pie—and use the larger amount of flour. In a small bowl, stir together the granulated sugar, flour, cinnamon, and salt. Sprinkle the sugar mixture over the fruit and toss gently to coat the peaches evenly. Set the peaches aside.

Pour the filling into the pastry-lined pie pan. Distribute the cubes of butter evenly over the filling. Roll out the second pastry disk the same way into a round at least 11 inches in diameter and 1/8 inch thick. Gently lay the round over the filled pastry, then trim the edge to match the overhang of the bottom layer. Fold the overhang either over itself or under itself to create an edge, sealing the edge securely and fluting it for an attractive appearance.

Brush the top crust with the cream, then sprinkle it with the turbinado sugar. Cut at least 6 large slits in the top crust to allow the steam to vent during baking. Cover the edges with foil or a crust protector if needed to prevent overbrowning.

Line a baking sheet with aluminum foil and place the pan on the lower rack of the oven to catch drips as the pie bakes. Place the pie on the center rack above the pan and bake for 50 to 60 minutes. Check the crust after 40 minutes. If the edges are not the same color as the exposed top of the crust, remove the edge cover. When the filling is bubbling and the crust is evenly browned, the pie is ready.

Let the pie cool completely (this will take at least 2 to 3 hours) on a wire rack before serving, then cut into wedges to serve.

Cook's Note: Put any rolled-out pastry trimmings on a baking sheet and sprinkle with sugar and cinnamon. Bake in a preheated 400°F oven for 10 to 15 minutes, until golden brown. Enjoy with a glass of cold milk for some down-home comfort food!

NATURAL AND DANGEROUS GRASSES • By Mas

Weeds flourish everywhere and anywhere on our farm, even in the bed of my pickup truck where dirt collects and early spring rains soak hidden seeds. But I have learned that many weeds are benign; they simply dry up in our summer heat. My father worried about the weeds, so I tried to appease him by reframing what I considered a weed. I called them natural grasses, a term that had a softer, more accepting tone. It also required a leap of faith by us and trust in our observations: not all weeds are evil.

My grandmother named weeds. She used the term *abunai kusa*, or dangerous grass, especially for Johnsongrass, a voracious weed that grows densely, sucks up water and nutrients, and crowds out other plants, including trees and vines. My grandmother didn't need a scientific experiment to verify how bad this weed was: she trusted her intuition based on experience and memory. I inherited her language. She was right: Johnsongrass is evil and dangerous.

PEACH MELBA

SERVES 4 TO 6

The week before I started college at UC Berkeley, I was fortunate to spend two days helping out in the pastry kitchen at Chez Panisse. We had been shipping our peaches to the restaurant for years and I had only gotten to visit once. Of course, I was nervous. In less than sixteen hours of work, I burned a tray of cookies and tripped down a flight of stairs as I carried hand-carved chocolate shavings of the best chocolate I had ever tasted in my life. Despite my mishaps, Alan Tangren, the then-head pastry chef, shared his kitchen with great kindness and generosity. He taught me how to pick out the ripest berries (blackberries, boysenberries, raspberries). He told me to look closely and focus on the tiny spheres that make up a single berry. The ones with the most intense flavor have a dull look rather than a shiny veneer. These ripe berries also look taut and ready to explode. Because this recipe has so few ingredients, it's critical that every element be at its best. But if fresh raspberries are unavailable, frozen ones can be substituted. Serve with gingersnaps for added crunch.

Nikiko

1   cup fresh ripe or thawed frozen raspberries

2   tablespoons turbinado sugar

1   tablespoon pure lemon extract (see note)

    About 1 pint vanilla bean ice cream

2   soft peaches, peeled, halved, pitted, and sliced

    Gingersnaps, for serving (optional)

In a food processor, combine the raspberries, sugar, and lemon extract and pulse until the sugar has dissolved. Pass the raspberry mixture through a fine-mesh sieve placed over a bowl, pushing it through with the back of a spoon. You will end up with a silky sauce. The sauce can be stored in an airtight container in the refrigerator for up to 1 week.

Scoop the ice cream into serving bowls and add a few peach slices to each serving. Drizzle about 1 tablespoon raspberry sauce over each bowl. Serve at once with gingersnaps.

Cook's Note: You can buy lemon extract, of course, but it is easy to make at home. Using a vegetable peeler, remove long, narrow curls of lemon zest from 1 lemon. Put the curls in a jar, add vodka to cover, cap the container, and leave to infuse in a cool spot. The longer the mixture sits and the higher the ratio of lemon zest to vodka, the stronger the lemon flavor will be. We start with zest strips from 1 lemon and 3/4 cup vodka and let it stand for two weeks.

PEACH-LEMONGRASS GRANITA

SERVES 4 TO 6

Granita is a fancy word for an icy frozen dessert. It is similar to *raspados*, flavored shaved ice, Mexican style, or a crunchy version of sorbet. The textured ice crystals make this a good choice as either a dessert or a palate cleanser. I have found that the double scraping is key to making the granita light and airy.

Nikiko

1   cup water

1/2 cup sugar

4   (4-inch) pieces lemongrass

4   gushy large peaches, peeled, pitted, and quartered

1/4 cup freshly squeezed lemon juice

In a saucepan, combine the water, sugar, and lemongrass, place over medium-low heat, and heat, stirring occasionally, until the sugar has dissolved. Remove from the heat and let steep at room temperature for 30 minutes. Remove and discard the lemongrass.

Put the peaches in a blender and blend until pureed. Pass the puree through a fine-mesh sieve placed over a bowl. Add the lemongrass syrup and the lemon juice to the bowl, stir well, cover, and refrigerate for 1 hour or so, until thoroughly cooled.

Pour the peach mixture into a shallow baking pan or dish; the mixture should be about 2 inches deep. Place the pan in the freezer for 2 hours, until the top and sides have solidified a bit. Using a fork, break up the solidified pieces into smaller ice crystals. Return the pan to the freezer and leave until frozen solid. This should take 6 to 8 hours.

Remove the pan from the freezer. Drag and scrape the fork through the frozen mass to create icy, fluffy flakes. You can serve the granita right away in small bowls, but I recommend that you return it to the freezer until just before serving because the granita tends to warm slightly and lose a bit of crunch when fluffing. You can also portion the granita into serving bowls and keep those in the freezer until you are ready to serve.

CHAPTER FIVE

Harvest Memories
PRESERVES and LEGACY

*"Preserving peaches is a practice of memory.
Preserves ask us to remember those who came before
in our all-too-often nameless food chain."*

—NIKIKO

Preserving Peaches Starts Here / BY MARCY

M Y MOTHER GREW UP before and during the Great Depression on a Wisconsin dairy farm where she learned how to make the most out of plentiful farm-fresh products for daily meals and how to preserve the remainder for enjoying throughout the year. Her neighbors called her the "food-preservation expert" because she canned, dehydrated, pickled, and froze all kinds of foods every year, from fruits (jams, jellies, chutneys, applesauce, leathers) and vegetables (sauerkraut, pickles, chowchow) to meats (sausages, headcheese, bacon, jerky) and dairy products (cheeses, butter, ice cream, noodles). She also shared her expertise with others, young and old alike. Mom was the local food-preservation project leader and state resource for 4-H clubs in Wisconsin, California, and Arizona (states in which she lived for more than twenty-five years each) and for many years taught courses in food preservation at two community colleges, training generations of food-service personnel, homemakers, and farm enthusiasts. With that type of expertise in the family, I couldn't have possibly grown up without learning a few things myself!

The truth about preserving foods for me is that while nothing is better than a high-quality fresh product, good preserved foods are far better than poor-quality and off-season not-so-fresh products. Although consumers have allowed the food industry to do most of the work in this era, the quality of the products and the options have become extremely limited in the marketplace. For example, it can be difficult to find peach jam in our local supermarkets, and commercial frozen peaches are beautiful but lack deep flavor. So if you have access to great-quality fresh peaches, I believe that you are better off bringing home a lot of them and putting in a little time preserving them—canning, jamming, freezing, drying—to enjoy at a later date.

I fear that the art of preserving food in the home kitchen is near extinction, and I am happy to share with you, my fellow peach lovers, what has become intuitive for me. The recipes in this chapter are a few of the favorite ways we preserve peaches on our farm at the peak of season. We have simplified the instructions for home cooks who may have never attempted to preserve food before, and though we realize that some of the methods may require resources that you do not have at hand, others will be possible to make for anyone with a stove, a pot, and some jars and lids.

CANNED PEACHES

MAKES 4 PINTS

If you have never canned—or "jarred"—before, please know that it is a lot easier than you think! If you are fearful about canning and would like to try it, find a friend, relative, or resource person with expertise (maybe through your county cooperative extension office, master food preservers program, or Slow Food colloquium) who can demonstrate how to do it and thus demystify the process for you. Another option is to turn to the many books, blogs, and websites that provide information on canning. For example, the *Ball Blue Book of Preserving* is a fantastic traditional source of good information about canning and freezing foods from one of the most longstanding canning-jar companies. For canning equipment, visit your local hardware store, antique shop, and/or online source.

There are two basic methods of canning peaches: the open-kettle or hot-pack method and the cold-pack method. The open-kettle method calls for heating or cooking the fruit or jam on the stove before sealing it in hot, sterilized jars and processing. The cold-pack method calls for putting cold fruit and syrup or brine (depending on the recipe) in hot, sterilized jars and then processing them in a boiling-water bath for a specified longer length of time. Certain low-acid foods require pressure cooking, which is not necessary for peaches. The boiling water bath is usually done in a canner, a large kettle fitted with a wire rack. Sterilizing jars and processing them for the specified length of time is essential to ensure safety. Because I want a more consistent product, full jars of fruit, and don't want to heat the kitchen longer than I have to, I use both methods at various times. Trouble can arise if you decrease the amounts of sugar, salt, or acid (vinegar or lemon juice) or cut the cooking time. If you have dietary restrictions that require you to consume less sugar, salt, or acid (depending on your recipe), be sure to consult a good professional resource on cooking technique and processing time to ensure food safety.

Marcy

4	cups water
2	cups sugar
16	to 20 peaches with give or soft peaches
1	tablespoon citric acid (optional)

Combine the water and sugar in a 6- to 8-quart nonreactive stockpot or Dutch oven and bring to a boil over medium-high heat, stirring to dissolve the sugar and create a light syrup. Turn down the heat to medium-low. Meanwhile, peel, halve, and pit the peaches and leave them as halves or cut into 3/4-inch wedges or chunks. As the peaches are cut, slide them directly into the hot syrup in the pot. If you are working quickly, the peaches will not discolor from oxidation before

they are in the syrup. If you are working slowly or want to prepare the peaches ahead of time, submerge them in a large bowl of water with the citric acid (or other commercial produce protector such as Fruit Fresh).

When all the peaches are in the syrup, simmer them gently until they are heated through. They are ready when their color is uniform and a toothpick or fork tines slide through them with no resistance. The timing will vary depending on the size and ripeness of the peaches, but they should be ready in about 10 minutes.

Meanwhile, sterilize your canning jars and lids (not the rings). Put them in another stockpot or large saucepan, add enough water to cover, and place over high heat with the cover on. When the water is boiling, lower the heat to keep the jars hot for at least 10 minutes.

Just before the peaches are ready, using rubber-tipped tongs, remove the jars, one at at time, and lids from the hot water and stand them upright on a work surface. Then, using a slotted spoon, lift the peaches out of the syrup and arrange them, cavity side down, in a jar, filling to within 1/2 to 1 inch of the rim. Ladle in the syrup, filling to within 1/2 inch of the rim. Wipe the lip of the jar rim with a clean, wet cloth to remove any bits of fruit or syrup, then top with a flat lid and loosely screw on a threaded ring. Roll the filled jar on its side to release any air bubbles that might be caught in the peach cavities and then turn the jar upright. Remove the ring band and lid to see if the level of syrup has dropped and add more syrup if needed to fill to within 1/2 inch of the rim. Then replace the lid and ring, firmly tightening the ring. Repeat the jar-filling process until you have used all your peaches or filled all your jars. If you run out of peaches and have extra syrup, it's okay if the last jar is only half full of peaches and filled with syrup.

{CONTINUED}

{CONTINUED FROM PAGE 135}

Place the filled jars in a canner with a wire-rack insert and fill with enough warm water to cover the jars by at least 1 inch. Cover the canner and heat over high heat until the water boils. Lower the heat to medium and boil gently for 20 minutes.

Using rubber-tipped tongs or a jar lifter, carefully remove the jars from the hot water. Leave the jars upright on a cutting board or cooling rack to cool. As the jars cool, you might hear the lids pop. That's good because it means they are sealing. After the jars have cooled for several hours, check to see if the seal is good on each jar by pressing on the center of the lid. If the lid moves up and down, it is not sealed, and you should eat the peaches right away or store them in the refrigerator and consume them within 2 months. If the lid does not move and is concave, it has vacuum sealed and the jar can be stored in your pantry for up to 1 year.

Cook's Note: If you don't have a canner with a rack insert, you can use a large pot with a deep colander or pasta insert. It is important that the jars not sit directly on the bottom of the pot, and that the pot is deep enough to submerge the jars fully in boiling water without the water escaping over the rim of the pot. Put the colander insert in the pot, put the filled jars in the colander, add water to cover by at least 1 inch, and proceed as directed if using a canner.

If you have excess syrup from simmering your peaches, don't pour it out! It is peach nectar at this point. You can strain it, pour it into sterilized jars, and process it along with your peaches. Or, you can use it to make Summer Sangria (page 35), Peach Margarita (page 41), a smoothie, iced tea, or any other beverage you like. It will keep in the refrigerator for about 2 weeks or for up to 1 year if processed and sealed in sterilized jars.

PEACH JAM

🎃 MAKES 3 HALF-PINTS

Every summer we have a Jamfest in our farmhouse kitchen to which we invite friends for a late night of jam making and movin' and groovin' to a combination of rock 'n' roll oldies and modern pop. (Song selection depends on who's stirring the pot!) We fill dozens and dozens of jars with jam made according to a low-sugar recipe ($4^1/_2$ cups peaches to 3 cups sugar) that calls for commercial pectin to ensure batch to batch consistency and to minimize the time required to cook the jam. Commercial pectin is available in most supermarkets and the recipe and instructions come with the package.

For those who don't want to use commercial pectin, I offer the following simple recipe. The essential element of good jam is the use of extremely ripe fruits, what we call gushers. To prepare the peaches, work in batches, pulsing the peaches in a food processor until chunky or passing them through a food mill or grinder. If you like, add flavorings or other fruits to the pot.

Marcy

$3^1/_2$ cups peeled and mashed, ground, or coarsely pureed soft or gushy peaches (6 to 8 peaches)

2 cups sugar

1 tablespoon freshly squeezed lemon juice

Pinch of salt (optional)

1 tablespoon unsalted butter (optional)

Combine the peaches, sugar, lemon juice, and salt in a deep, wide nonreactive Dutch oven or stockpot and bring to a boil over medium-high heat, stirring to dissolve the sugar. Once the mixture has reached a boil, turn down the heat to medium or medium-low. Cook, stirring frequently with a flat-bottomed wooden spoon or spatula to ensure the jam does not stick to the pot bottom, for 20 to 40 minutes, depending on how thick you want the jam to be. If foam develops on the surface of the fruit, add the butter, which will minimize foaming. The jam is ready when it coats the back of the spoon. Remove the pan from the stove.

While the jam is cooking, begin to sterilize your canning jars and lids (not the rings). Put them in another stockpot or large saucepan, add water to cover by a couple of inches, and place over high heat. When the water is boiling, lower the heat to keep the jars hot for at least 10 minutes.

{CONTINUED}

{CONTINUED FROM PAGE 137}

Just before the jam is ready, using rubber-tipped tongs, remove the jars and lids from the hot water and stand them upright on a work surface. Fill the hot, sterilized jars with the hot jam to within 1/4 inch of the rim. I use a metal measuring cup to transfer the jam from the pot to the jars. As you fill each jar, wipe the lip of the jar rim with a clean, wet cloth to remove any bits of fruit, then top with a flat lid and firmly screw on a threaded ring. The USDA recommends that you process the jars in a boiling-water bath for 15 minutes (see page 136). I know a lot of experienced canners who do not process, but I would not recommend that to ensure food safety! After processing for 15 minutes, remove the jars and let cool for several hours. The lids should seal while cooling. To test if a seal is good, press on the center of the lid with your finger. If the lid moves up and down, it is not sealed, and you should refrigerate the jar and consume the jam within 2 months. If the lid does not move and is concave, it has vacuum sealed and the jar can be stored in your pantry for up to 1 year.

If you prefer to skip the canning jars and lids and pantry storage, you can simply transfer the cooked jam to clean, lidded containers and store them in the refrigerator. The jam will hold for about 2 months.

Cook's Note: Sometimes I freeze the 3 1/2 cups fresh peach puree needed for this recipe, then make the jam at a later date. I have noticed that the jam thickens much faster on the stove top when I use thawed frozen puree rather than fresh puree. In both cases, the jam will have thickened more once it has cooled.

The Night Shift / BY NIKIKO

IN MID-JULY between nine and ten o'clock in the evening, the throbbing summer sun finally tucks itself beyond the coastal mountains west of the Central Valley. My feet, still swollen from standing outside most of the day, slowly begin to pulse back to their normal size. The dark brings a small respite from the heat, but this reprieve doesn't mean we sleep long luxurious hours in the cool of night. Instead, we start our second job: it's the perfect time for peach preservation.

Before our night shift starts, regardless of how late it is, we refuel and take a much-needed dinner break. Prior to my dad coming in—he's almost always the last one—my mom and I exchange glances and check the clock. We set a benchmark time because we never eat until everyone has arrived: by a certain hour, if we don't hear dad's old pickup roaring toward the house or see a trail of dust kicked up from one of our tractors on its way back to the shed, one of us has to go convince him that he needs to come home. In a family business, voluntary collective punishment is one of our strongest negotiating tools.

We usually see his dusk-lit frame and hear his heavy work boots trudging toward the house before the family farm collective bargaining ensues. I know we're off the hook as soon as I hear the outside faucet gush a cool river of water and his familiar washing-up sounds: gulping, spitting, spurting water out of his nose to get the dirt out, and deep sighs. We can momentarily rest.

So far, only once have I come in later than my dad. One summer, I misjudged how long it would take to finish working the ground in a fallow field. That day, my tractor was pulling a piece of equipment, what we call the weed crusher, that we had borrowed from a neighbor. Desperate to finish the field and thus spare myself a few hours of work in the heat, I made two final passes along its length. By the time I finished, I could barely see the front of the tractor. I knew I was in trouble.

Dragging the weed crusher home required careful calculation of the rocks, borders, and cement valves that lined the avenue. Hitting a valve would be deadly and require many hours of repair. Luckily, I had my cell phone in my pocket. Using the faint light the moon casts and the blue glow from the phone's artificial rays, I slowly crept home. I squinted into the dim light and used the only other navigation tools I had with me to signal the way home: my memory of the route, the mental maps of the small divots and potholes that line our dirt roads, and the sound of rocks and soil that lay on different stretches of the path. That night, for the first time, my mom had put a benchmark time on me.

After our late-night dinners and showers, we pull out pots and pans, buckets of peaches, paring knives, and the puree attachment to our old blender. Then we crank up the heat: we boil canning jars and shiny metal lids in one pot and the thick peach puree made from our best gushers of the day in a second pot. We always make at least three big batches of jam in a night.

On the other side of the farm, my *baachan* (grandma) sleeps. She has already put in decades of night shifts with my *jiichan* (grandpa). Now, she uses the cool mornings to "put up" her peaches in simple syrup and freezes them in bulging plastic pouches. Every summer she makes enough to last for the rest of the year. Before my *jiichan* died, every morning they would eat a heaping spoonful of peach preserves on top of hot bowls of oatmeal. When I lived with them after college, I often shared their morning routine. Against the hearty oats, the peach preserves burst on my tongue. The texture brought me back to the heat, sweat, and satisfaction of summer harvests when we can taste the results of a year of hoping and working.

When my *jiichan* grew old, I believe that eating peach preserves every morning helped him remember what he had created and sustained as long as his body allowed: a family farm worth preserving. The year he died, my *baachan* worried about not being able to finish all the preserves that she had prepared the previous summer for the two of them. I told her not to worry, that as a family we'd help eat last summer's harvest. We shared the burden of loss by filling our bodies with food memories meant for my *jiichan*.

Our farm owls must think we're their nocturnal cousins. The barn owl cuts silently through the fields like a ghost: the shimmering white body dashes between the bright moon and the dark earth in search of a meal. With much less grace than the birds, we also thrust ourselves into our night shift. Like them, we capture food treasures in the dark and stillness of summer nights. We clang metal pots, hum with the sound of puree, and blurt out estimated "jarring" times like cranky short-order cooks. We work together to fill and seal jars of golden orange summer quickly.

Making peach preserves on our farm is about family labor. It's a ritual of optimism, futurity, and haunting. We steal the night to transform fresh peaches into memories, hoping to preserve an essence of what was once alive. When we're done, dozens of jars cool on our dining-room table. I'm tired. But as I trudge home, I feel fulfilled. I know that in a few months, those jars will be magical: each one a small time capsule that allows us to taste the past. But it's not just the past summer's peaches that I recall when I open a jar. It's my *jiichan* too. Peach preserves give me another way to remember him.

PICKLED PEACHES

When I was a kid, we had a single peach tree in our backyard orchard that produced more than enough peaches for our family of five. My mom taught us to preserve the peaches, which is how I learned how to make these pickled peaches. They are a nice accompaniment to pork roast, Thanksgiving turkey, grilled or roasted chicken, or your favorite Indian or lentil dish. This is one recipe in which you can use small cling peaches and keep them whole or you can use halved or quartered freestones. This recipe works best if you use uniformly sized peaches or peach pieces, and it is a great way to use up a batch of small peaches.

Marcy

3	cups sugar
2	cups distilled white vinegar (5 percent acidity)
1	cup water
6	(3-inch) cinnamon sticks (optional)
18	whole cloves (optional)
6	to 8 pounds soft freestone or small cling peaches

In a large nonreactive stockpot, combine the sugar, vinegar, water, cinnamon, and cloves and bring to a boil over medium heat, stirring to dissolve the sugar. Meanwhile, peel the peaches. If using freestones, halve or quarter and pit them; if using small clings, leave them whole with the pit inside. Turn down the heat to medium-low and gently add the peaches to the syrup and spices. Let the peaches heat through in the hot syrup, but do not them boil. This should take 10 to 15 minutes, though the timing will depend on the ripeness and size of the peaches. They are ready when a toothpick or fork slides through them with no resistance.

Meanwhile, sterilize your canning jars and lids (not the rings). Put them in another stockpot or large saucepan, add water to cover, and place over high heat. When the water is boiling, lower the heat to keep the jars hot for at least 10 minutes.

Just before the peaches are ready, using rubber-tipped tongs, remove the jars and lids from the hot water and stand them upright on a work surface. Then, using a slotted spoon, lift the peaches out of the syrup and arrange them, cavity side down in the case of the peach halves, in a jar, filling to within $1/2$ to 1 inch of the rim. If you like the appearance and spiciness,

{CONTINUED}

{CONTINUED FROM PAGE 141}

add 1 cinnamon stick and 3 cloves to the jar if using pint jars or 2 cinnamon sticks and 6 cloves if using quart jars. Ladle in the syrup, filling to within 1/2 inch of the rim. Wipe the lip of the jar rim with a clean, wet cloth to remove any bits of fruit or syrup, then top with a flat lid and loosely screw on a threaded ring. Roll the filled jar on its side to release any air bubbles that might be caught in the peach cavities and then turn the jar upright. Remove the ring band and lid to see if the level of syrup has dropped and add more syrup if needed to fill to within 1/2 inch of the rim. Then replace the lid and ring, firmly tightening the ring. Repeat until you have used all your peaches or filled all your jars. If you run out of peaches and have extra syrup, it's okay if the last jar is only half full of peaches and filled with syrup.

Place the filled jars in a canner with a wire-rack insert and fill it with enough warm water to cover the jars by at least 1 inch. (See the Cook's Note on page 136 for an alternative to a commercial canner.) Cover the canner and heat over high heat until the water boils. Lower the heat to medium and boil gently for 10 minutes.

Using rubber-tipped tongs or a jar lifter, carefully remove the jars from the hot water. Leave the jars upright on a cutting board or cooling rack to cool. As the jars cool, you might hear the lids pop. That's good because it means they are sealing. After the jars have cooled for several hours, check to see if the seal is good on each jar by pressing on the center of the lid. If the lid moves up and down, it is not sealed, and you should eat the peaches right away or store them in the refrigerator and consume them within 2 months. If the lid does not move and is concave, it has vacuum sealed and the jar can be stored in your pantry for up to 1 year.

If you prefer to skip the canning jars and lids and pantry storage, you can simply transfer the cooked peaches and syrup to clean, lidded containers and store them in the refrigerator. The peaches will hold for about 2 months.

PEACH CHUTNEY

This is an old family recipe from my mother who made this chutney as a young adult in Wisconsin. Ironically, it includes both peaches and raisins, both of which our family grows today. Some people use golden raisins because they don't like the color of dark raisins. I prefer dark raisins because they are less processed, and are not treated with sulphur dioxide. Serve as an accompaniment to pork roast or chops, steak, or grilled chicken. Jars of homemade chutney also make wonderful gifts.

Marcy

2 quarts peeled and finely chopped peaches with give (about 20 peaches)

³/4 cup raisins

¹/2 cup chopped yellow or white onion

2 cups light brown sugar

2 tablespoons mustard seeds

2 cups cider vinegar (5 percent acidity)

1 tablespoon ground ginger or peeled and grated fresh ginger

1 teaspoon salt

Combine all the ingredients in a large nonreactive stockpot or Dutch oven, place over medium-low heat, and cook slowly, stirring periodically to prevent scorching on the pot bottom, for about 40 minutes, until the juices are reduced by about half and the chutney becomes thick like a jarred salsa.

While the chutney is cooking, begin to sterilize your canning jars and lids (not the rings). Put them in another stockpot or large saucepan, add water to cover, and place over high heat. When the water is boiling, lower the heat to keep the jars hot for at least 10 minutes.

Just before the chutney is ready, using rubber-tipped tongs, remove the jars and lids from the hot water and stand them upright on a work surface. Ladle the hot chutney into the hot, sterilized jars, filling to within 1/4 inch of the rim. As you fill each jar, wipe the lip of the jar rim with a clean, wet cloth to remove any bits of food, then top with a flat lid and firmly screw on a threaded ring.

Place the filled jars in a canner with a wire-rack insert and fill it with enough warm water to cover the jars by at least 1 inch. (See the Cook's Note on page 136 for an alternative to a commercial canner.) Cover the canner and heat over high heat until the water boils. Lower the heat to medium and boil gently for 10 minutes.

Using rubber-tipped tongs or a jar lifter, carefully remove the jars from the hot water. Leave the jars upright on a cutting board or cooling rack to cool. As the jars cool, you might hear the lids pop. That's good because it means they are sealing. After the jars have cooled for several hours, check to see if the seal is good on each jar by pressing on the center of the lid. If the lid moves up and down, it is not sealed, and you should eat the peaches right away or store them in the refrigerator and consume them within 2 months. If the lid does not move and is concave, it has vacuum sealed and the jar can be stored in your pantry for up to 1 year.

If you prefer to skip the canning jars and lids and pantry storage, you can simply transfer the cooked chutney to clean, lidded containers and store them in the refrigerator. The chutney will hold for about 2 months.

BREAKING THINGS • By Mas

I always hope that things break in convenient places. We use old equipment on the farm; often it's all we can afford. Also, considering the amount of energy required to build something new, old equipment is very environmentally responsible. Used equipment is "green" as well. But equipment often gets smashed and shattered. When my father was alive, equipment I broke was magically repaired by his welding and parenting skills. He'd say little, never yelled or questioned me, and instead simply recognized what needed to be fixed. It has taken me years to learn how to weld well enough to repair things—and equally as long to become a good father.

PEACH-TOMATO SALSA

I have enjoyed putting up fruits and vegetables ever since I learned from my mother back in the mid- and late 1960s. I can remember canning while she and I listened to radio reports of the race riots during the hot August nights of 1965 and 1968—yes, those were *hot* August nights. Now, in the midsummer when we have loads of peaches, I still enjoy canning at night as we "put away" the summer bounty.

I often double this recipe so that we can enjoy it all year. We use it on eggs or breakfast burritos in the morning or with tacos, tostadas, burritos, or chiles rellenos for lunch or dinner. This versatile salsa is medium-hot. If you like your salsa hot, see the note that follows for suggestions. Look for chipotle chiles in adobo sauce in Hispanic groceries or in the Hispanic food section of well-stocked supermarkets. Select soft but not gushy peaches for this recipe, preferably a variety that remains firm when exposed to heat, like Elberta.

Marcy

5	cups peeled and chopped soft peaches
1	tablespoon freshly squeezed lime juice
	Juice of 1/2 lemon (1 to 2 tablespoons)
2	cups peeled and chopped fresh tomatoes or diced canned tomatoes
1	large green or yellow bell pepper, seeded and diced
1/2	large orange or red bell pepper, seeded and diced
1	cup diced yellow or white onions
1/4	cup diced jalapeño chiles, seeds and membranes removed (see page 67)
2	cloves garlic, chopped
1/4	cup coarsely chopped fresh cilantro
1/2	cup white vinegar (5 percent acidity)
1/2	cup tomato sauce
6	tablespoons tomato paste
2	to 3 tablespoons honey

In a large nonreactive stockpot or Dutch oven, combine the peaches, lime juice, and lemon juice and toss to coat. Add the remaining ingredients (use the larger amount of honey if your peaches are not very sweet), and stir well. Place over medium heat, bring to a boil, and cook for 3 to 5 minutes, stirring frequently. Lower the heat to a simmer and cook for about 30 minutes, until the vegetables are fully cooked, the liquids are reduced, and the salsa is the thickness that you desire. The thicker your salsa gets, the more you will need to stir it and scrape the bottom of the pot so it does not burn.

Meanwhile, sterilize your canning jars and lids (not the rings). Put them in another stockpot or large saucepan, add water to cover, and place over high heat. When the water is boiling, lower the heat to keep the jars hot for at least 10 minutes.

Just before the salsa is ready, using rubber-tipped tongs, remove the jars and lids from the hot water and stand them upright on a work surface. Ladle the salsa into the hot, sterilized jars, filling to within 1/4 inch of the rim. As you fill

- 1 teaspoon cayenne pepper or red pepper flakes
- 1½ teaspoons ground cumin
- ¾ teaspoon salt
- 1½ teaspoons adobo sauce from canned chipotle chiles (optional; adds heat and smokiness)

each jar, wipe the lip of the jar rim with a clean, wet cloth to remove any bits of food, then top with a flat lid and firmly screw on a threaded ring.

Place the filled jars in a canner with a wire-rack insert and fill it with enough warm water to cover the jars by at least 1 inch. (See the Cook's Note on page 136 for an alternative to a commercial canner.) Cover the canner and heat over high heat until the water boils. Lower the heat to medium and boil gently for 10 minutes.

Using rubber-tipped tongs or a jar lifter, carefully remove the jars from the hot water. Leave the jars upright on a cutting board or cooling rack to cool. As the jars cool, you might hear the lids pop. That's good because it means they are sealing. After the jars have cooled for several hours, check to see if the seal is good on each jar by pressing on the center of the lid. If the lid moves up and down, it is not sealed, and you should store the jar in the refrigerator and consume the salsa within 2 months. If the lid does not move and is concave, it has vacuum sealed and the jar can be stored in your pantry for up to 1 year.

If you prefer to skip the canning jars and lids and pantry storage, you can simply transfer the cooked salsa to clean, lidded containers and store them in the refrigerator. The salsa will hold for about 2 months.

Cook's Note: If you want a milder or hotter salsa, adjust the amount of jalapeño chile, cayenne pepper, red pepper flakes, and/or adobo sauce. If your salsa is too spicy hot, add more tomatoes and/or peaches.

FROZEN PEACHES

Freezing is by far the easiest way to preserve peaches for the off-season. Once you've done it the first time, you'll never buy frozen peaches again. Freezing your own gives you the power to choose only the best, fully ripe peaches. However you use the peaches later, such as in pies or smoothies during fall, winter, and spring, you'll be able to enjoy them at their peak.

Nikiko

Select soft or gushy peaches. Depending on how many peaches you are freezing, line 1 or more baking sheets with parchment paper. (The slices from 2 peaches usually fit on one 15 by 12-inch baking sheet.) Peel, halve, and pit the peaches, then cut into 1/2-inch-thick slices. Arrange the slices on the parchment-lined pan, placing them close together but not touching. Put the pan in the freezer.

When all the slices are frozen solid, transfer them to zip-top bags and seal closed. Return them to the freezer and use them before next year's harvest.

Letting Go: The Death of an Old Farmer
/ BY MAS

Y FATHER DIED in the spring of 2010.
He was neither famous nor wealthy. He was quiet and hardworking—a good man with a shovel in his hands. When we lose our fathers, we lose a buffer between death and our own mortality.

My father suffered a major stroke in 1997, but through hard work and therapy, he recovered adequately—and even relearned how to drive a tractor. I realized we had switched roles. I was the teacher and he was the student.

A second major stroke in 2003 knocked him off his feet. My mother became his primary caregiver. We all did the best we could. Yet I began to dread the ring of the phone late at night.

A third and final stroke took him. In his last moments, I held his rough hands. Throughout the years, they continued to manifest the many years in the fields with old, ingrained calluses.

He was strong and independent with a stubborn streak that was both his strength and weakness. He willed himself to recover after each setback, yet struggled when he needed assistance. Finally, he had to accept help and we were fortunate, as not everyone does.

Shame may be the reason he wanted to be left alone. He deserved more but resigned himself to the fact that growing old was lonely. He had support around him. My mom dedicated her life to his care—my father would not be alone. We tried to acknowledge his need for autonomy and self-respect. He didn't want to be a burden.

Mom faced an impossible situation: Dad was not going to get better. She labored daily with commitment. She prolonged his life with love and care. Her hands maintained his dignity and enabled him to pass peacefully. My mother could do no more. In our fast-paced and youth-oriented world, her emotional loyalty was rarely acknowledged or rewarded. Caregivers bear this burden, as if it's a penalty to take care of someone aging and gradually declining. My mother shared the spirit of the caregiver—a corps of devoted individuals too often invisible and neglected.

Despite all the years of time and effort, when my father was gone, my mother quietly said, "I'm going to miss taking care of Dad." If I could muster half as much love in my heart, I would be blessed forever.

Dad was a farmer. He grew savory peaches and sweet raisins on an eighty-acre family farm. I don't recall him ever saying he loved us. He was a stoic man who spoke through his caring actions.

Emotions were implied and unspoken—and clear in my memory. As a child, I remember him picking me up and carrying me after I tripped on a vineyard wagon tongue and split my lip and broke a tooth. When I was a teenager, he quietly rescued me without anger when my tractor got stuck in the mud and I needed his help to free the equipment and me.

During his final years, he wore the public stolid face of an old dying farmer. We all knew he still cared about life. He spent hours looking out the window at his family farm.

As he gradually declined and could no longer work in the fields, Mom gave me a stack of his work clothes. The first time I wore them I could still smell a hint of his sweat—a gentle, sweet aroma, a working-class scent. Work was his life, and in the end, when I walked our fields, I realized his spirit was now part of the farm.

The final years were a challenge for all of us. I realized how unprepared I was for the inevitable. I lacked wisdom and struggled to create systems to care for an aging parent. Few organizations and community structures were in place to help: I lacked the social and cultural infrastructures to adequately adjust as Dad declined.

Death would probably be easy, dying was the hard part.

His decline took a toll on our health, especially my mother's, his primary caregiver. The challenge of care and commitment was overwhelming, yet sadly expected. I often thought of the thousands of other caregivers, laboring in silence, suffering in their own ways, still wanting to believe caring for a loved one was a privilege.

Dad knew he had become a burden. He struggled with his own self-respect. Part of his dignity was lost, although we sometimes found meaning in the little things that had become the hardest to endure. Dad loved getting a bath and he looked like a kid, scrubbing himself with his good left hand, smiling as a stream of warm water danced off his head. Yet going to the bathroom was a daily struggle to maintain that sense of worth.

Some of the most basic aspects of life were hard. When we ignore their significance, we devalue their importance and we foster a culture of denial.

It's time caregivers tell their personal stories. By sharing intimate stories publicly, they acquire new meaning—a type of legitimacy, a validation of the labor of love.

Caregivers should know that they are not alone. Growing old is not a secret, and dying should not be hidden in whispers. It's easy to lose dignity when life is lost in seclusion.

I stayed up with my father the last night of his life. We had called hospice and they helped tremendously with pain management during his final weeks. Dad was suffering but still had some self-respect.

Some claim that at the very end of life, there's a burst of energy, a final surge of activity— life's finale. That final night, Dad sat up and wanted to stand.

I helped the old farmer onto his shaky legs and he rose for a few minutes. Then he could no longer hold himself up and sat, leaning on the side of the bed. I was next to him and told him it was okay. Exhausted, he leaned on me. Silently we sat in the dark. I could hear and feel his rapid breaths. He sighed. I patted him on the back. I asked if he wanted to lie down again and he nodded.

He lay peacefully as I watched him sleep. It was a role reversal: As a father, he had once watched over his sleeping son. Now it was my turn.

The next morning, Nikiko flew home from graduate school to see her grandfather. Her intention is to take over the farm one day.

One of Dad's final acts of life was to see his granddaughter. He reached out and grabbed her hand and held it. He gave a soft laugh, patted her hand, and rolled over. Perhaps somehow he understood and was passing the farm on to the next generation, the next farmer who was planning to work these fields of gold.

I had made a promise to keep my father on the farm as long as I could. Over a decade ago, while recovering from this first stroke, we made a pact: I'd bring him back to the farm and he would never leave. We were very fortunate that circumstances allowed us this opportunity. In the end, with family gathered around his bed, he died in his farmhouse. Promises made, and gratefully, promises kept. He could leave in peace.

Death was not a passive act—we were all witness to his life at that moment. It will take years to process it fully, but I sensed both a loss and an opportunity.

I no longer have a living father, yet I will always remember him. With the gradual loss of warmth in his body, it was okay to miss him.

DRIED PEACHES

Most dried peaches available for purchase are dried halves. The Masumoto method of drying yields a very different result: paper-thin slices with explosive flavor. The key to this method is overripe peaches, triple-digit daytime heat, cool mornings, and the bit of concrete that borders our house and pool. I contend that the partial rehydration of the slices overnight and the second dose of sunlight the next morning create a curing effect that imparts an umami quality as the flavor concentrates. The result is a whimsical skinny dried peach slice. These peaches are incredible in my mom's Rolled Pork Loin (page 83) and are a great grab-and-go snack. Although we use and reuse plastic dehydration screens because we dry peaches throughout the summer, you can achieve the same effect by using parchment paper.

Nikiko

For equipment, you will need a mandoline or similar slicer, such as a Benriner Japanese slicer; fine-mesh plastic or wire dehydration screens or parchment paper and baking sheets; and cleaned square plastic garden trays or cardboard boxes that can be inverted and used as base for the screens.

Select very ripe soft or gushy freestone peaches. This method will not work with peaches with give; they must be riper. Check the weather report to make sure that the day you will be drying the peaches will be in the triple digits. (See the note on page 154 if you live in a more temperate climate.) Then, the day before you plan to dry the peaches, store them in the refrigerator overnight. This helps them hold their structure and makes them easier to slice.

Halve and pit the peaches. Set your mandoline to cut thin slices no more than about 1/8 inch thick. Have your screen(s) ready, or line your baking sheet(s) with parchment paper. To slice each peach, hold it cut side down and slide it across the blade, being careful to keep your fingers curled safely away

{CONTINUED}

{CONTINUED FROM PAGE 153}

from sharp edge. A safety word to the wise: instead of trying to slice the very last bit of the peach half, eat it as your reward for being cautious and/or wear cut-resistant gloves!

Place the slices on the screen(s) or the parchment-lined pan(s). It is okay if their edges touch, but do not allow them to overlap. Put the flipped garden tray(s) or cardboard box(es) outside in direct sunlight over a hot, clean surface, like cement, and place the screen(s) or pan(s) on top. (On our farm, we have found that we must put the peaches outdoors by four o'clock in the afternoon or there will not be enough direct sunlight and the slices will oxidize.) The direct sunlight and triple-digit heat will seal the outside layer of the slices so their color remains bright and golden.

Leave the peaches out overnight. The dew and cooler temperatures of the morning will rehydrate the slices slightly. Let the slices dry again in the morning sun. (Don't despair if your weather doesn't reach triple digits. This method will also work if the temperature is above 90°F, but you will probably need to leave the peaches out for two nights, instead of one.) The peaches are ready when they are completely dry to the touch. They should also pop off the screen or paper with a gentle tug.

Enjoy the dried peaches immediately, or store the slices in sealed zip-top bags in the freezer for several months. It is important to eat these peaches slowly to allow the flavor to release gradually on your tongue as you chew.

Cook's Note: If you don't live in a dry, hot climate like we do, you can prepare the peaches the same way and dry them in a commercial dehydrator.

Leaving Behind Stories / BY MAS

Dear Children,

When I die, what will I leave behind for you? The things I cherish are stories and memories: the breakfast on the porch; a farm walk; sharing the first ripe peach of the season, the juices running down your faces. We lived in a world rich in details and authentic emotions—memories alive and embedded in a story. That's the legacy I hope to leave.

What will forever be a part of my story? The land. Yet our farm isn't full of huge profits. As I've grown older, I've come to realize it is not success that I want to leave behind. Rather, it is significance. I want to be remembered as someone who loved and worked the earth and hope to keep the farm a farm. Imagine forever altering the landscape by keeping it the same: a farm that retains its identity in a region holds on to a piece of the region's history. To know who we are because we still have a sense of where we are.

I want farms to show where food is grown and remind people that places still matter. Future generations may want to see and feel that story and know where their daily nourishment comes from. Open spaces have a magical quality. Imagine for a moment standing in the sunshine and breathing in the air; see the green of nature and smell the freshness of spring or ripeness of summer; long to taste something real and honest. A family farm is not much different from an old-growth forest or a historical site: a sacred place, a voice shouting that we count, we matter.

Farm memories are buried in the land, dreams live in my fields. My hope is to romance the next farm generation. There's something important here—an activism in the fields. Grow food and be radical, raise a family out in the country and keep something right.

Leave behind a memory and keep alive a story of significance.

Your dad

ACKNOWLEDGMENTS

W E GROW A LOT OF THINGS ON THE MASUMOTO FAMILY FARM: peaches, nectarines, grapes, weeds, wildflowers, summer gardens, field mice, stories, recipes, to name a few. But there are many things that the farm grows in *us*. Gratitude and humility top that list. We sincerely want to thank the many who have helped us with this literary cookbook.

Nikiko thanks:

I'm not sure it is possible to pause and say thank you enough to my coauthors Marcy and Mas (Mom and Dad) and to Korio, my brother. They are the awesome trio I am thankful to see every day. I am grateful for my visionary and tenacious dad, Mas, without whom this cookbook would never have been conceived. My partner in the kitchen, Marcy, is my favorite person to cook with. She taught me the foundation of all I know about cooking, the most important of which are love and fearlessness. Thanks to my brother, Korio, for being a force of calm and levity; I know I would have higher blood pressure without you.

I want to thank my *jiichan,* Takashi "Joe" Masumoto, who is no longer with us, and my *baachan,* Carole Yukino Sugimoto Masumoto, for starting and sustaining this farm. There would be no Masumoto peaches without them.

Throughout the history of our farm, teams of workers have come and gone. I wish there was a way to adequately acknowledge every person who has given sweat and time to work these fields. I am humbled.

When harvest is at full speed, there is a whole "off-farm" team of people the farm depends on to find homes for our fruit. To the whole team at Pacific Organic Produce, I adore you all. Greg, Stevie, Cindy, John, Elizabeth, Amy, Jason, and Kate, I am so lucky to work with you every summer.

Deep thanks to the institutions who have shepherded our peaches for years from farm to eater: Brandt Farms, Hubert Cold Storage, Kimura Trucking, Fuji Melon, Berkeley Bowl, and Chez Panisse. The farm is lucky to have so many champions of our fruit, including long-time friends and supporters Alice Waters, Bill Fujimoto, Glenn Yasuda, and Karen Beverlin.

A huge bouquet of gratitude to the team at Ten Speed, especially to Jenny Wapner for opening the door to this project, Melissa Moore for her generous guidance and friendship, and

Toni Tajima for her humor and design prowess. Thank you to so many others who have worked diligently to create food adventures in Ten Speed cookbooks: Aaron Wehner, Sharon Silva, and Kelly Snowden. Thank you to Rick Bayless for taking the time to share such a beautiful peach memory with us and the world.

Thanks to the whole photo team who captured our peach dishes more beautifully than I could have imagined. Karen Shinto and Vicky Woollard, your cooking skills, endless positivity, and attention to detail put you in rock-star status. Karen, I learned so much from watching the grace and speed with which you worked. I am thankful to Staci Valentine for sharing so much time and talent to capture beautiful moments of the farm, recipes, and peaches. Thanks to the entire photography team: Douglas Axtell, Ethan Sharkey, Amber McKee, and Amy Paliwoda. I am so grateful for your sweat (literally)!

Thanks to Estel Salcido and Marie DiBona-Herzog for helping me prepare for the photo shoot. You have taught me that beauty surpasses style; it's an outlook and way of being. You both embody that. A very special thanks to my friend and coach, Renata Razza, for supporting me to love peaches and life with radical joy and unbridled courage.

Lessons I have learned from culinary giants and friends Jim Dodge, Kristine Kidd, and Jesse Cool are sprinkled throughout this cookbook. Thank you for sharing your wisdom and inspiring us with your work!

Infinite thanks to my dear friends who tested recipes with care and honesty: Nicole Gurgel, Katelyn Wood, Kyle Schultz, and Elizabeth Davis. I wish I could share meals with you all the time.

Finally, to the friends, family, and community who have shared meals brimming with peaches and encouraged me to farm, cook, and write, I am so grateful to share a table with you. I work to grow the perfect peach every season because I love eating with you.

—Nikiko

Marcy thanks:

I would like to thank the many friends and colleagues who provided positive reinforcement and those who helped by testing my recipes, including Amanda Hopkins, Lisa Sugimoto, Susan Fisher, Regina Vukson, Cecelia Rudolph, Ginny Boris, Shin Tanaka, Gwen Soltero, Pat O'Lague, Suzanne Hissong, Marge Matoba, Debbie Tom, and Liz Hathaway. Thank you all so much for your time—shopping, cooking, testing, and providing helpful comments. Thanks also to the many family and friends, too many to name, who taste-tested many of the dishes while under development and provided feedback. A special thank you to Estel Salcido and Marie DiBona-Herzog for bolstering my confidence. Finally, a special thanks to Nikiko, Korio, and Mas for their constant willingness to try what Nikiko and I had prepared for "just one more taste test."

—Marcy

Mas thanks:

I want to thank and acknowledge the publications where versions of some of these stories and essays were first published. Thanks to the *Fresno Bee* and Jim Boren for the opportunity to write a monthly column, to Heyday Books and Malcom Margolin, and also Free Press and Leslie Meredith. Also huge thanks to Elizabeth Wales.

A very, very special thanks to Rick Bayless for taking time to write the foreword and for being a friend who does understand peaches. Also to Molly O'Neill and other "foodies" who engage with our farm story.

Thanks to the many at Ten Speed Press, including publisher Aaron Wehner, and a special hug to our editor Melissa Moore who supported us throughout the project, and Toni Tajima with her design vision. A huge thanks to Karen Shinto and Vicky Woollard. Also thanks to Sharon Silva and Jean Blomquist. And a very warm thanks to Jenny Wapner who originally connected with us as we started this work.

Special thanks to our photographer Staci Valentine for her energy and spirit along with Douglas Axtell for his wise support, and thanks to the photo shoot team of Ethan Sharkey, Amber McKee, and Amy Paliwoda.

And finally a warm thanks to all who support our family farm. You do complete our farm.

—Mas

To learn more about the Masumoto Family Farm, visit www.masumoto.com

INDEX

MEASUREMENT CONVERSION CHARTS

VOLUME

U.S.	IMPERIAL	METRIC
1 tablespoon	1/2 fl oz	15 ml
2 tablespoons	1 fl oz	30 ml
1/4 cup	2 fl oz	60 ml
1/3 cup	3 fl oz	90 ml
1/2 cup	4 fl oz	120 ml
2/3 cup	5 fl oz (1/4 pint)	150 ml
3/4 cup	6 fl oz	180 ml
1 cup	8 fl oz (1/3 pint)	240 ml
1 1/4 cups	10 fl oz (1/2 pint)	300 ml
2 cups (1 pint)	16 fl oz (2/3 pint)	480 ml
2 1/2 cups	20 fl oz (1 pint)	600 ml
1 quart	32 fl oz (1 2/3 pints)	1 l

TEMPERATURE

FAHRENHEIT	CELSIUS/GAS MARK
250°F	120°C/gas mark 1/2
275°F	135°C/gas mark 1
300°F	150°C/gas mark 2
325°F	160°C/gas mark 3
350°F	180 or 175°C/gas mark 4
375°F	190°C/gas mark 5
400°F	200°C/gas mark 6
425°F	220°C/gas mark 7
450°F	230°C/gas mark 8
475°F	245°C/gas mark 9
500°F	260°C

LENGTH

INCH	METRIC
1/4 inch	6 mm
1/2 inch	1.25 cm
3/4 inch	2 cm
1 inch	2.5 cm
6 inches (1/2 foot)	15 cm
12 inches (1 foot)	30 cm

WEIGHT

U.S./IMPERIAL	METRIC
1/2 oz	15 g
1 oz	30 g
2 oz	60 g
1/4 lb	115 g
1/3 lb	150 g
1/2 lb	225 g
3/4 lb	350 g
1 lb	450 g

ABOUT THE AUTHORS

MARCY THIELEKE MASUMOTO

As co-owner of the Masumoto Family Farm, Marcy Masumoto has been responsible for the selection of peach varieties and for the development of recipes and peach products and is actively involved in the farm's management and in seasonal fieldwork. With the help of her children, Nikiko and Korio, she hand packs the farm's specialty peaches each summer. She has cooked with many different peach varieties, perfecting recipes and methods of working with large quantities of tree-ripened fresh peaches. Much of what she knows today she credits to growing up on a family goat dairy, where she learned how to cook, bake, and preserve foods at an early age.

Off the farm, she has worked in the fields of health and education, initially as a nutrition advisor. She currently works at the Central Valley Educational Leadership Institute at California State University, Fresno, which focuses on improving education in central and rural California. She holds a bachelor's degree in health education with a minor in nutrition from Loma Linda University, a master's degree in community development from University of California at Davis, and a doctorate in educational leadership from UC Davis and Fresno State University.

In addition to her work on and off the farm, Marcy enjoys entertaining, gardening, and cooking in the family's farmhouse kitchen.

NIKIKO MASUMOTO

Nikiko Masumoto is a feminist farmer, agrarian artist, and community leader. Born in California's Central Valley, she spent her childhood slurping overripe peaches on the family farm and never missed a summer harvest. In 2007, she graduated with the highest honors from the University of California at Berkeley with a degree in gender and women's studies. It was there that she realized she wanted to return to the valley to farm. But first, she completed a master of arts in performance as public practice at the University of Texas at Austin. Her area of research focused on the performance of memory and Japanese American history (specifically the movement for redress). For her thesis, she created a one-woman show called *What*

We Could Carry, based on the testimony given in the 1981 redress hearings. In June 2011, she moved back to Del Rey, where she lives with her grandmother and spends her days in the fields, apprenticing under her father. Off the farm, she also enjoys traveling, eating, and yoga.

DAVID MAS MASUMOTO

David Mas Masumoto is a third-generation farmer and the author of six books, *Wisdom of the Last Farmer*, *Heirlooms*, *Letters to the Valley*, *Four Seasons in Five Senses*, *Harvest Son*, and *Epitaph for a Peach*. He is currently a columnist for the *Fresno Bee* and *Sacramento Bee* and was a W. K. Kellogg Foundation Food and Society Policy Fellow from 2006 to 2008. His writing awards include a silver medal from the Commonwealth Club of California, the Julia Child Award for best literary food writing, and the James Clavell Literary Award. He was also a finalist for the James Beard Award for best food writing, and *Wisdom of the Last Farmer* was named the Best Environmental Writing in 2009 by the National Resources Defense Council. Masumoto received the Award of Distinction from the University of California at Davis in 2003 and the California Central Valley Excellence in Business Award in 2007. He is currently a board member of the James Irvine Foundation and the Public Policy Institute of California and has served as chair of the California Council for the Humanities. In 2013 he was appointed to the National Council on the Arts. Learn more at www.masumoto.com.

Library of Congress
Cataloging-in-Publication Data is on
file with the publisher

Hardcover ISBN 978-1-60774-327-9
eBook ISBN 978-1-60774-328-6

Design by Toni Tajima
Food styling by Karen Shinto
Food stylist assisting by
Vicky Woollard
Photography team: Douglas Axtell,
Ethan Sharkey, Amber McKee
Prop styling by Amy Paliwoda

Printed in China

10 9 8 7 6 5 4 3 2 1

First Edition